Introduction

It may surprise some, but the
Manchester City, founded ma. ,
quite a history. It is nevertheless a well-chronicled history, a
rollercoaster ride with many a bump along the way.

Formed from the ashes of St. Mark's and Ardwick Association
Football Club, the Citizens have seen it all. Titles, cup triumphs,
relegations, promotions, scandals, many, many kits, a few
grounds and even a variety of club badges to boot. A club that
managed to get relegated as league champions has always done
things differently, sometimes for the better, sometimes not.

When we (Simon Curtis and Howard Hockin) got together and
came up with the idea that eventually became this book, we
wanted to take another look at some of City's biggest moments
over the past few decades, both good and bad; to examine the
days that helped define the club as it exists today, one of the
biggest clubs in the world.

So we decided to revisit these days by creating our own
minute-by-minute reports. It was a fascinating experience to go
back to days we thought were embedded in our memories, to
discover there was so much more to the days than we thought
we knew. We chose ten matches in all, because it's a nice,
round number and most importantly, it divides by two.

Some younger supporters of the Boys in Blue may be surprised
to learn that City haven't always had a great team, and
sometimes we did "give in". We felt it important therefore that
this book wasn't just a list of City's greatest days, but that it also
took a look at some of the club's darker moments, the days

we'd rather forget, but which we're going to remind you about anyway. What doesn't kill us only makes us stronger, after all. It was those dark days and those lean times that made what followed so special to so many. We'd earned it after all, and have the grey hairs and heart conditions to prove it.

We didn't just want to look at the match itself, so this book is about more than the 90 minutes of blood, toil, tears and sweat. And own goals. No, we thought it important to take you back to look at the club as it was at that time, on and off the pitch. To look at the context of each match, the implications of the result and the club as it existed at the time. If you're lucky we'll even throw in some weather reports too. It's a look at how the match may have been reported at the time by those that were paid to talk about the beautiful game.

The ten matches are in chronological order, which means a few tears in the opening chapters. But don't worry, happier times follow, and we think you'll like the ending. We hope you get as much joy out of the book as we did researching and writing it. So sit back and re-live the epic semi-final replay against Spurs in 1981, the heart-breaking defeat to Luton in 1983, the thrashing of Huddersfield, the remarkable play-off final of 1999, the Spurs cup comeback, drink in the greatest moment of our history and more.

Enjoy.

Simon Curtis & Howard Hockin

Thursday 14th May 1981
FA Cup Final Replay 1981: Manchester City v. Tottenham

"Villa. And still Ricky Villa. What a fantastic run. He's scored!!"

Welcome to Wembley Stadium, for the second time in five days. We have the small matter of trying to decide the outcome of the Centenary FA Cup Final today, on a warm, balmy London evening, it must be said.

Many questions remain unanswered: Can Spurs up their game? Can City's amazing spirit lift them once more? Will we see the real Ricky Villa tonight instead of the hunch-shouldered apology of last Saturday? Can Ossie's dream come true? Will Chas and Dave ever stop singing that horrid song?

This and much, much more to come this evening from Wembley, where we await the team news for this eagerly anticipated cup final replay. Not since Chelsea-Leeds in 1970 has the final gone to a second game and never before has one taken place at Wembley. Chelsea and Leeds, remember, replayed their final at Old Trafford after a 2-2 draw under the Twin Towers.

The attendance tonight will be just under the mythical 100,000 that saw Saturday's entertaining draw between the two sides. For security reasons, night games have a reduced 92,000 capacity. There will be more Spurs fans than in the first game, as tickets have been on open sale in London and obviously have been snapped up eagerly by Tottenham supporters. However, it has to be said that the tunnel end is already jam packed with City fans, who have swamped the motorway and the train lines south again today to back their side. There were queues stretching right around Maine Road when tickets went on sale on Monday and, if anything, the atmosphere is more partisan tonight because of the increased numbers of fans of the two sides present. A really electric atmosphere building as we await team news from the two camps.

City's main doubt appears to be young Dave Bennett, the striker who has a thigh knock. He was doubtful for the first game, but shook off the problem in time to take his place and played a big part in the opening goal on Saturday. If he hasn't made it, Dennis Tueart will most likely step in. Tony Henry is likely to be sub once again.

Tueart will be itching to play after having crossed words with John Bond about being left out of the original line-up. Here is what he had to say:

"I'm available in whatever capacity the manager wants me and he knows that. I don't have to spell out how eager I am to help this club at Wembley. My attitude is already well-known. I desperately want City to win."

So, after seemingly missing out on his Cup Final dream, Tueart stands ready to play after all. This just a week after the infamous Daily Mirror headline "You Can Go, Tueart!" broke upon us, seemingly signalling the end of his illustrious Manchester City career. John Bond's reply was simply to say "Tueart? I feel more sorry for Tommy Booth", referring to the experienced defender's absence, his place at the back going to Tommy Caton, after netting the 5th round winner at Peterborough. This of course is the drama of such occasions. Some play, some don't and many are disappointed.

Kevin Reeves (bruised ribs) and Gerry Gow are both announced as less than 100% at present too and were undergoing fitness checks this afternoon. We will soon know the outcome of these.

As for Spurs, the major doubt is whether Ricky Villa will be trusted to start or not. If manager Keith Burkinshaw saw enough in a poor performance at the weekend to put him in again, then Gary Brooke will remain substitute. If not, the youngster may well start. Villa, it must be said, cut a totally forlorn figure as he trudged off towards the tunnel in tears after being substituted last weekend. Winger Tony Galvin, who played a big part in keeping Spurs chugging forward despite a below-par team performance in the first game, is also doubtful after picking up a slight knock.

Quick reminder how the two protagonists got here this evening: CITY beat Malcolm Allison's Palace 4-0 at home, Norwich 6-0 at home, then fourth division Peterborough 1-0 at London Road, then two titanic tussles with Everton, 2-2 at Goodison and 3-1 at home in the replay (the two games watched by a total of over 100,000 fans) and finally the drama-soaked extra time win over Ipswich at Villa Park. SPURS meanwhile drifted gently past QPR after a draw in the 3rd round, beat Hull (h) 2-0 in the 4th round, Coventry 3-1 at home in round 5, then little Exeter were dispatched 2-0 at White Hart Lane in the quarter finals. The Hillsborough semi-final with Wolves was drawn 2-2 and needed a Highbury replay to see them through easily enough (3-0) in the end, with a wonder goal from Ricky Villa that night, remember.

What have the two managers to say? First up, here's Keith Burkinshaw: "I want people to be talking about the 100th Cup Final for years to come. My very last words to the players before they leave the dressing room will implore them to do full justice to themselves and to their club. I want to see them play the kind of football we all believe in at Spurs. I don't enjoy dull, defensive football and we are not equipped to play it."

John Bond appears to agree with his Spurs counterpart: "I can't predict an outcome nor would I try. I just want us to put on a show that is exciting, exhilarating and full of the good things about the game of football. I would almost say that the quality of football will be as important for me as the result. I think I would sooner lose a cracking match than lose a boring one."

Well, both managers talking the talk there. Whether it's all hot air or not, we will find out shortly. City reputedly on £10,000 a man and Tottenham on £7,000 to win this game tonight, so the extra incentive, if it were needed, is there.

19:15 Team news has arrived and there is a shock. Dave Bennett has made it into the side ahead of Dennis Tueart. Bennett was said to be touch and go, but he makes it and Tueart will have to be happy with a place on the bench ahead of Tony Henry, who drops out altogether. For Spurs, Villa keeps his place ahead of Gary Brooke. The only other change is a numerical one, with Steve Perryman and Ricky Villa swapping numbers 5 and 6. Don't ask.

So, City with three Scotsmen and eight Englishmen line up like this: **Corrigan: Ranson, McDonald, Caton, Reid; Power, Gow, Hutchison, Mackenzie; Reeves, Bennett - Sub Henry.**

Spurs can count on six Englishmen, a Scot, two Irish and of course two Argentineans: **Aleksik: Hughton, Miller, Perryman, Roberts; Ardiles, Galvin, Hoddle, Villa; Crooks, Archibald - Sub Brooke.**

1925 Two things are certain this evening: firstly there will be a winner tonight. Penalties will follow at the end of extra time, if they are needed and secondly Tommy Hutchison will not be a part of them. The two goal man – having scored at both ends on Saturday – has ruled himself out of any penalty shoot-out here tonight. The Scot last missed a penalty for Scotland against Spain in a World Cup qualifier in 1974 and hasn't taken one since...

"I resigned my position as penalty taker that day and I have no ambition to make a name for myself now," he tells us. Some might say you have already made a bit of a name for yourself becoming only the second ever player to score for both sides in a Cup Final, Mr Hutchison, but let's not split hairs.

1935 And out of the tunnel into blinding late evening sunshine come the two teams, once again led proudly by the managers John Bond and Keith Burkinshaw. A little wave here, a little glance around there. And those glances will reveal a jam packed tunnel end, awash with sky blue flags and banners. A really cracking atmosphere here tonight. At the far end and indeed down the sides too, a great swathe of Tottenham support bellowing their welcome too. Shouts of "City! City!" mingle with "Glory Glory Tottenham Hotspur". It fair makes the hairs stand up on the back of your neck.

The teams have lined up in traditional manner below the royal box and are being introduced to his Royal Highness the Prince of Kent and his wife.

The City bench has taken its position and very calm they look in their blue suits. Bond, assistant John Benson and physio Roy Bailey at the front with John Sainty. I can see Dennis Tueart the substitute alongside Dr Norman Luft and those missing out just behind, a disappointed Tony Henry, alongside Phil Boyer, Glyn Pardoe and Tommy Booth. There's some cup fighting pedigree in those last two alone.

Teams are kicking in, getting a feel of the ball before the off, giving the two goalkeepers a little practice and soaking up the terrific atmosphere being created by these two sets of supporters.

1945 All ready to go. The sight of Glenn Hoddle, shirt out, shorts hiked high on his hips, swinging his arms ready for action will bring fear into the hearts of City supporters. His free kick it was, of course, that bounced in off Tommy Hutchison's shoulder for the equaliser on Saturday, but it is Hoddle who had scored in all four of the sides' previous encounters before the final too.

City get us underway then, playing from right to left, in other words attacking the Spurs support in the first half. Referee Keith Hackett once again gets us firing, with Hutchison and Reeves kicking off.

01:00 Blistering start to the Cup Final, with the ball fairly pinging around. Spurs looking more lively than at the weekend already, but City's midfield tigers doing their usual job, as Mackenzie and Gow go steaming in on Ardiles for the first foul of the game. Ardiles rolls out of play, gets up quickly and the little number 7 is hopping about in some pain. And just to give you an idea of the super-charged atmosphere here tonight, Mr Hackett blew for the foul some ten seconds ago and the players are still tussling for the ball on the edge of the City box, some fifty yards from where the foul was committed. Nobody heard the whistle in this incredible din.

It was a double scissors from Gow and Mackenzie, but referee Hackett has decided Gerry Gow is the one he wants to talk to and is giving him a firm piece of his mind. Whether the frizzy-haired Scot can hear him or not is another matter. No booking anyway, Gow backs off to prepare for the free kick to Spurs and the tunnel end reverberates to "Gerry Gow, Gerry Gow, Gerry Gow". We can only imagine what the Spurs fans are singing.

02:00 Spurs prove they have some tackling capacity too, as Graham Roberts scythes down Kevin Reeves for a City free kick midway into the Tottenham half. Roberts gets up and barks some instructions. Clearly missing a tooth or two, the Spurs man looks as frightening as anything City have out there tonight. Kick is taken short to Ray Ranson, who feeds Tommy Hutchison down the right wing and he wins the game's first corner off the back-tracking Tony Galvin. Paul Power bends it in with his left foot towards the near post where Tommy Caton and Kevin Reeves are waiting. The ball flicks out to Steve Mackenzie, whose firmly struck shot bounces away off Chris Hughton in the box.

03:00 City keeping up the early pressure, just as they did on Saturday, winning a second corner. Taken by Power again, it comes out to the edge of the box and Reeves is fed through the inside right channel, but is blocked by Ricky Villa of all people just as he was shaping to shoot. Another corner and a shaky offside trap not functioning properly for Spurs there. Villa well aware of what he had to do, tracked back and put his foot in at just the right moment. That will have helped him forget Saturday's woes a little.

04:00 Same pattern developing as last time out. Early City pressure and aggression. Spurs sitting back and soaking it up, wanting to play those angled long balls from Hoddle out of defence for Archibald and Crooks to chase. The crowd is loving it.

08:00 Goal! Tottenham! The early breakthrough that didn't come at the weekend falls to Spurs. Trickery from Ardiles, as he skips several tackles on the edge of the box, then feeds it through to Archibald, whose shot is baulked by Joe Corrigan. The ball squirms loose to Ricky Villa on the edge of the six yard box and he buries it past Joe Corrigan for only his 5th goal of the season. Suspicion of offside from some angles, but the angle that matters is that of Keith Hackett. What a start here.

The replay shows us just how good that run from Osvaldo Ardiles was and also the little slice of luck for Spurs, as Archibald's shot hits Tommy Caton and falls back into the path of Ricky Villa. What a transformation of fortune for the Argentine, who only on Saturday looked anything but fit for purpose for another match of this magnitude. **Tottenham 1 Manchester City 0**

10:00 Wow, the equaliser! City make it 1-1 straight away and it's an absolute belter. Ranson's long free kick, after an innocuous-looking challenge out on the right, is headed out by Miller, then Roberts, but falls to Hutchison, who nods it down into Mackenzie's path and his sweet right foot volley is the sharpest thing you'll see today. It fair arrowed into the top corner. One of Wembley's finest. And now it's the tunnel end's turn to go berserk. Mackenzie, it must be said, is one of the English game's sweetest strikers of a ball and there is little doubt he hit that one just plum. **Tottenham 1 Manchester City 1**

11:00 Hoddle hits the post with an outrageous free kick. Nicky Reid adjudged to have handled. Hoddle's free kick swerved round the wall and hit the right hand post as Corrigan sprawled for it. What a close shave for City now. This game is on fire. Can anyone remember a cup final starting to such gay abandon? Terrific stuff from both sides.

15:00 First Tottenham corner after a concerted period of pressure ends with a shot from Archibald looping well wide off Ray Ranson. All comes to nothing as Roberts is penalised for climbing all over Ranson as the ball comes in.

19:00 Dave Bennett is charging towards the goal as Aleksik comes rushing out and stops his progress. He has, however, drifted beyond his markings and handles outside the box. Moment of consternation as Mr Hackett deliberates whether punishment beyond a free kick is due, but he errs on the side of caution and Aleksik gets away with it. Five man wall, six if you include the loitering Kevin Reeves and it's touched short to Paul Power's left foot, but – unlike in the semi final against Ipswich – Power's shot sails high and wide.

23:00 A little bit of the early sting has gone out of the game in the last few minutes. Spurs seeing plenty of the ball, looking livelier it has to be said, with Hoddle, Ardiles and Villa very much to the fore. The Spurs faithful responding with a throaty rendition of "He'll take more care of you, Archibald, Archibald". City trying to find their rhythm through Gow and Hutchison in midfield, but Reeves has looked a little isolated up top so far.

25:00 Free kick to City out on the far touchline. Good closing down by City, keeping Spurs pinned back in that corner. When the throw in was taken, referee Keith Hackett decided there was some backing in by Crooks on Caton and City can swing one into the area. It's a dangerous one from Hutchison, which reaches Reeves's head at the near post, but Garth Crooks is back to head wide of his own goal for a corner as the flick on careers across the face of goal.

29: 00 Close shave Spurs! Hoddle tries to chip Crooks in but Nicky Reid heads out. It goes straight to Ricky Villa, whose cannonball shot strikes Corrigan and knocks the big man over. He put his fists up instinctively but I'm not sure he knew too much about it. Saturday's man of the match in crucial action once again here. Unorthodox goalkeeping from Corrigan but equal to anything he produced on Saturday.

32:00 First City break of note for a good few minutes, led by Power and Reeves but it peters out at the edge of the Tottenham area as Bennett stays rooted instead of running onto Power's defence-splitting pass. Spurs have been getting the upper hand, with Hoddle, Villa and Ardiles stronger in midfield than Mackenzie, Gow and Power at the moment. Gerry Gow just not getting through the incredible amount of tracking and harrying that he did at the weekend.

36:20 City working their way back into it, but are exposed down the right flank with McDonald caught up-field. Ricky Villa runs on to another accurate long ball from Glenn Hoddle and whacks a shot into the near post, where Corrigan is again down athletically to touch it round the foot of the post.

39:00 Another good chance for Spurs! Galvin with the quick throw in releases the livewire Villa, who turns Nicky Reid inside out before centring to Garth Crooks. His vicious left foot drive zips past Corrigan's near post. "You're worse than Garry Birtles" whoops the tunnel end, but in truth that was quite close to 2-1 Tottenham.

40:00 First yellow for City. It's Tommy Caton, with a carbon copy of his manoeuvres on Garth Crooks on Saturday. Crooks turns quickly onto Perryman's forward ball and Caton just goes straight through the Spurs man. The young City defender wasn't quick enough to go with the darting movement of Crooks and that is the story of this first half so far.

The free kick eventually falls to Crooks, who blasts it way over.

41:00 Another Spurs break ends with Galvin running wide onto a decent feed from Archibald as City are caught short at the back a little and his shot is blocked by Corrigan, by far the busier of the two keepers now, and it's Ray Ranson first to the rebound, before Tony Galvin can cause anymore havoc.

45:00+1 Referee Keith Hackett blows for half time and it's Tottenham 1 Manchester City 1 in a game that has hardly stopped from the 1st minute to the 45th.

Half Time Analysis: Tottenham will be pleased to have put in a much better performance than at the weekend. More bite, quicker to the ball, sharper in the pass, they have been galvanised by the skills and passing range of Glenn Hoddle and the selfless running of Villa and Archibald.

City have Steve Mackenzie to thank for being level at the interval. One of Wembley's greatest ever goals bringing City back to parity here. In truth Mackenzie and his midfield colleagues have not had the same grip on this one as they did on Saturday. Perhaps those legs of Gerry Gow are a little tired after all his efforts in the first game. Power and Hutchison too have been peripheral figures in that intensely contested area of midfield.

As the two sides head off down the tunnel, it's the Spurs fans in full voice, no doubt happy to see that their side has turned up tonight. The two managers leave side by side, with John Bond flapping his arms. Looks a little frustrated if you ask me. Nevertheless all still to play for at one-one. City will need to be quicker into the tackles second half and relieve some of the pressure on Joe Corrigan, who has been by far the busier of the two goalkeepers.

Second half about to get under way. Hold onto your hats, ladies and gentlemen.

46:00 And it's City straight into their stride. Two misplaced passes from Spurs allow Hutchison to open up those long legs and stride down the right. His cross in is met weakly by Reeves and it's cleared to the far side, where Bobby McDonald, the left back, puts in a great tackle in the far corner. City and McDonald well advanced right from the off here.

I feel it is my duty to tell you all that there's a pigeon on the pitch. He was there at half time had a little peck at the turf and he's back for more now, with the slight difference that there are twenty-two sets of studs stamping around him and 92,000 pairs of eyes watching him. Doesn't seem unduly bothered by the noise or the occasion though.

There's a corner to be taken by Spurs but we can't get it taken until our feathered friend is removed. He doesn't seem able to fly, which is unusual in a bird, so the reserve linesman is on and tucks him into his tracksuit top. That's the end of that.

50:00 PENALTY! Drama at the start of the second half. Penalty to City! Caton's long ball helped on with the aid of a back header by Kevin Reeves, sets David Bennett through and as he goes to shoot, Miller and Hughton sandwich him. Down he goes and there is no hesitation from the hitherto excellent Mr Hackett, who has called everything right so far, even the pigeon incident. Not wanting to put any pressure on Kevin Reeves here, but a penalty has never been missed in an FA Cup final at Wembley. Last one scored was, wait for it, for Tottenham in 1961. Dear me, the irony.

GOAL to City. No pressure at all for Reeves. An exemplary penalty into the corner makes it Manchester City 2 Tottenham 1. He hit it strong and low to Aleksik's left and it shot into the corner making the side netting bulge. Perfect accuracy and nerves of steel. Game on.

Now it's the tunnel end bubbling. What an atmosphere here now. And what a second half we have in store. Great spirit by City to fight back from that early goal and take the lead in the Centenary Cup Final. Arsenal are the last side to come from behind to win the Cup and that was against Liverpool ten years ago.

51:00 And Spurs getting a bit tetchy now. The normally ice cool Steve Perryman chooses to throw the ball in Paul Power's face as the throw goes against him. Mr Hackett has a quiet word with the Spurs captain as he wanders past muttering dark things to himself. Crowd is – predictably – in quite a lather now.

52:00 Really coming to the boil now. Spurs clearly unnerved at going behind. The tackles are flying in left right and centre. Ray Ranson is going to be booked for a foul on Villa. Both Argentineans imploring referee Hackett to take Ranson's name and address. Sure enough their politely persuasive English has done the trick and Ranson goes into the ref's note book. At the same time Gerry Gow is breathing into Garth Crooks' face and

Tommy Caton has gone to ground. Ranson looks non-plussed, but Perryman's arms are still pointing and flapping.

53:00 And another one into the book. That's three bookings now and two in a minute here, as Tony Galvin upends Tommy Hutchison and receives the yellow card. Hutchison in possession, chopped from behind. Clear booking for the Spurs man.

54:00 Danger for Spurs! Tempers are frayed and focus is also going out of the window. Reeves and Roberts tussling on the edge of the box, the ball pops up for Hughton to clear, but he slides it back towards Aleksik, not having seen Dave Bennett loitering with intent. His back pass has just enough woomph to carry through to the goalkeeper. Close call though. Can't take your eye off this for one minute.

56:00 Danger at the other end! Hoddle jinks inside his marker and lets rip with his left foot from twenty-five yards. Corrigan at full stretch to tip it over the bar. From the corner there's a scramble and Archibald's shot appears to strike McDonald on the arm. More protests from Spurs players but Mr Hackett's not interested. Well he is interested, in Archibald, who must have said something tasty in Gaelic, because he's following Ranson, Galvin and Caton into the little black book of shame. 4th booking of an increasingly fraught game here.

57:00 Off! Off! Off! chant the Tottenham fans, as Gerry Gow performs an elaborate reducer on Ossie Ardiles. The little Argentinean is very upset and there's a bout of shirt scrunching and curled lips between the two. Gow joins the others in the book, but it's yellow. The game in danger of bubbling out of control here. Foul after foul and the crowd is also fizzing now. Nothing like a bit of skulduggery to raise the temperature.

There's a fan on the pitch! As Mr Hackett wags his finger at Gow, they are approached by a Spurs fan who evidently wants to ask the City midfielder where he gets his hair done. It's not the time for that kind of small talk, however, and Bobby now has the miscreant in a tight headlock. Needless to say, the game has restarted already.

61:00 Bennett and then Reeves have shots blocked as City break through. Ball bounces off Roberts to safety. City seem to have ridden the immediate storm of Tottenham's indignation over the penalty.

66:00 Cheap foul given away by McDonald and Hoddle floats one in for Spurs. Roberts goes up to challenge Corrigan but it's a foul on the big keeper.

68:00 Power breaks free on his own into the Spurs half but is flagged just offside. There were four City on three Spurs defenders there for a second, but the through ball wasn't released on time. Brave performance this from City, taking the sting out of their opponents. You can see the midfield men have upped their contribution, with Power and Gow in particular really getting through some work. Halfway through the second half.

71:00 GOAL! Tottenham drag themselves level. All to play for again. Hoddle's delicate chip over the defence falls to Archibald, but as the ball bounces off his foot, Crooks nips in to toe end it past Corrigan. There was a penalty appeal against Caton in the immediate build up to the goal too, so Spurs will feel justified. 2-2, what a match we have now. It's on a knife edge.

Can't praise Hoddle's ball in too much. He chipped it like he was coming out of a bunker with the sand wedge, the ball held up perfectly on the grass, with a heavy backspin and just as Archibald was about to chase it down, Crooks dived in and "stole" his goal. Well, they've stolen 47 between them this season, so they have both had prodigious seasons. Spurs won't care who got it. The main thing is that they're level. Don't forget they've never lost a cup final, five out of five so far. Great noise around the old stadium now, as the darkness envelopes North London and the floodlights shine down on this rectangle of green where all the action is taking place. Terrific, all-consuming match we have here and it is coming nicely to the boil.

75:00 Can't hear myself think in this noise, so I'll just tell you what I can see. Villa down the right, pulls it across into the middle where Crooks takes a swing at it but Nicky Reid blocks bravely and the ball pings back out into that hotly contested midfield area. Beginning to think of extra time? Penalties? I'm beginning to feel for some of those players and their legs, remembering the spate of cramp attacks we had in the extra period on Saturday. There isn't a man out there tonight, who hasn't worked his socks off.

76:00 Oh. Lord. What. A. Goal. RICKY VILLA for Spurs!! With a snaking, unbelievable slalom effort to put the Londoners in dreamland. What a goal. A goal to grace any cup final, any football match and City's defenders are on their knees here, in a pile of utter despair. Dear me, what a football match we are witnessing here tonight.

It started with a City attack, believe it or not, which broke up and allowed Tony Galvin a long run down the left flank from deep inside his own half. He pushes it inside to Villa in a little space. The Argentinean turns and runs at the City backline. The run takes him past Caton, Reid and Ranson, back inside past Caton a second time and under the body of Corrigan. He is off on a celebratory run now that should see him past Marble Arch in about ten minutes. What a goal. It matches the marvellous strike by Mackenzie from earlier. My word that feels like hours ago now. We are in the noisy dark cauldron of night time Wembley and the whole place is in uproar. **Tottenham 3 Manchester City 2.**

12 minutes to hang on for Tottenham. 12 minutes for City to get it level yet again in this amazing final.

80:00 Substitute for City Hectic movements down on the benches, as Spurs fidget nervously and City get Dennis Tueart prepared to come on. The old warhorse, who has served City on and off since 1974, will get his taste of Wembley 81 after all, even if it looked like his goose had been cooked before the first game had even started. One of City's greatest post-war servants is stretching and readying himself for a last blast from the Blues to try and pull level. It's left back Bobby McDonald coming off. Boy, he looks tired, his shirt and shorts absolutely soaked in sweat. Tueart on the other hand looks wound up like a ball of string. On he comes. 10 minutes left on the clock. He approaches the two front men, David Bennett and Kevin Reeves and makes a gesture with his arms, as if to say "you two spread out a bit, I'm coming through the middle". So, three up front for City as they attempt to salvage something from this epic tie.

83:00 Spurs getting cocky, City getting desperate. Hoddle nutmegs Mackenzie as he comes in off the left wing, then pings his shot so high, even that pigeon that was with us earlier might have baulked at chasing it. Tueart meanwhile is organising furiously in the middle, pointing and gesticulating to team mates, who are tired and leg weary.

84:00 Graham Roberts powers a header wide from Hoddle's corner. Just think, a year ago he was a non-league player, now he stands six minutes from FA Cup final glory.

86:00 Dennis Tueart has the merest sniff of a chance, but he snatches at it as it falls from a heading duel in the box from Power's deep cross and the ball bobbles through to be collected by Aleksik. The night sky now filled with the piercing whistles of 50,000 Tottenham fans.

88:00 Wide open now with City pressing forward. Spurs find a gap and are away through Crooks, but as he approaches Corrigan, the big man smothers the ball for the umpteenth time. They are about to announce the Man of the Match for the two games combined and nobody has played better than Corrigan, that's for sure.

90:00 Sooo close City! It's Dennis Tueart again, this time even closer than his first effort. He gets a hold of a left foot shot from Reeves' knockdown and the ball bullets past Aleksik and his right post. Is that City's final throw?

90:00+2 AND THAT'S IT: ALL OVER AT WEMBLEY!! SPURS WIN IT IN THE YEAR OF THE COCKEREL. Thanks to the artistry of Ricky Villa, who scores one of Wembley's all-time great goals. Let's not forget Steve Mackenzie's effort for City, which on another day, would have been a worthy match winner itself, but it's Tottenham's day. Manager Keith Burkinshaw ambles onto the hallowed turf to begin his round of congratulations. A stunning game bookended by Ricky Villa goals. He opened the scoring. Spurs pulled back by Mackenzie's volley and a Kevin

Reeves penalty before Crooks and Villa with a masterpiece, tipped the scales towards the Londoners.

Nice touch as Steve Perryman gets his team mates organised for the walk up to the Royal Box to receive the cup from Prince Michael of Kent, little Ardiles gives a consoling hand to the giant City keeper Joe Corrigan, who has done more than most for City's cause out there over the 210 minutes.

Perryman it is that lifts the cup then. There's a little delay as he tries to put his medal down, but there it is. The cup goes to White Hart Lane. Perryman joined by an ecstatic fan now, who can't stop hugging him. His team mates troop past behind him. Miller and Roberts solid as you like at the back tonight, Villa looking chuffed to bits and keeper Aleksik who was steadiness personified. Among the hand-shakers in the Royal Box is Peter Swales, City's chairman, who is wearing the face of a man who has just swallowed a lump of coal, as he perfects a multipurpose smile that could mean anything at all. Ardiles is last up and the little man looks thrilled. What a part he has played along with his team mate Villa. The City players file through led by Power and Corrigan, who have performed heroically. Their faces are drained from the massive effort put in and as they descend those famous steps, they are faced with the sight of Ricky Villa in the most enormous and ridiculous paper hat covered in streamers and rosettes. How galling that must be.

Some stats just in for those of you who enjoy that sort of thing and can still focus properly:

<u>Free Kicks</u>: Spurs 15, City 17
<u>Off sides</u>: Spurs 4, City 4
<u>Shots</u>: Spurs 14, City 8
<u>On Target</u>: Spurs 10, City 5
<u>Corners</u>: Spurs 9, City 5
<u>Bookings</u>: Spurs 2, City 2

Let's see if we can grab a quick word with one or two of the protagonists out there tonight:

John Bond: "The fairy tale just didn't come true but I'm not dejected about it. The players did everything I asked of them and it's just the young lads like Ranson I feel sorry for…"

Ranson indeed is in tears down on the pitch now.

Bond again: "Joe was magnificent in goals in the two games and now that it's over, he's proving to be a magnificent man. Dennis Tueart might have saved us. He didn't get a hold of his first chance but he hit the second as sweet as a nut. But I reckon Spurs' name was on the cup when the season started."

And about Villa's winner "It was a magnificent goal but I bet if Keith Burkinshaw had been in my place, he wouldn't have said it was a good goal. He seemed to beat six or seven people in the space of four yards or so and the ball went through Joe's legs, or beneath his body into the back of the net. You score those sorts of goals once in a lifetime and it reinforced my view that we were never going to win it once it went to a second match. It was a good goal but Steve Mackenzie's volley was unbelievable." No bias there from the defeated manager.

He made mention there of Joe Corrigan. Well, some slight recompense for the City man, who has been awarded the BBC's

Man of the final trophy for his performances over the two games. Richly deserved.

What a night the two teams have treated us to, though. Top drawer entertainment from start to finish in a vibrant, passionate atmosphere that, after two games and a period of extra time, has finally delivered the 1981 FA Cup winners, Tottenham Hotspur.

City share the Cup glory

HEY labelled it "Ossie's Cup final" but it was his Argentinian amigo Ricardo Villa who turned Wembley into a personal platform for his skills.

**Hallelujah!
It's Final
pride for
Bond's men**

Tottenham 3 Man. C. 2

Saturday 14th May 1983
Division One. Manchester City v Luton Town

"And Stein again. And he gets the cross in. Williams has come. ANTIIIIIC!!! Oh it's there. Luton have done it!"

"Queen Mary reckoned that when she died and was opened, they'd find the word "Calais" lying on her heart. Whether they ever did is a matter for the historians, of course. When the time comes to open up Manchester City, it's a fair bet they will find, among other things, "Luton Town"", so writes the great Eric Todd in today's Manchester City versus Luton Town programme, referring not only to the momentous occasion we have before us this afternoon at Maine Road, but to some classic old encounters between the clubs, which include that most memorable game in 1961 where Denis Law scored six and the game was abandoned. It could only happen to City.

1200 It's a warmish day in Manchester but City fans will not be noticing the weather as three o'clock approaches, for the prospect of the club's first relegation in 17 long years is very real today. How has it come to this, football people will be asking themselves and indeed City fans are asking themselves the selfsame question. After last season's competent if unexciting 10th place finish and the drama of the centenary cup final the year before that in 1981, the arrival of Trevor Francis and all the other big signings, the ambition and the colour, the club finds itself, incredibly, right on the brink this afternoon.

Today's visitors, Luton Town, have of course their own survival to secure too. It is winner takes all at Maine Road and we will be bringing you the crucial developments as this nervy afternoon proceeds along its path.

1230 Just looking back at City's season. Quite incredibly they were top of the pile in September after starting the season with a bang. Three consecutive wins, at Norwich on the opening day and then at home to Stoke and Watford (the game where Bobby McDonald kept goal for 85 minutes of the 1-0 win), put City top. As recently as November, the home win over Southampton had City secure in 2nd spot in the table, dreaming of UEFA Cup qualification at the very least. That table – agonisingly for City followers - now looks like this with one game to go:

Sunderland	**49**
Notts Co	**49**
Coventry	**48**
Birmingham	**47**
Man City	**47**
--	
Luton Town	**46**
Swansea	**41**
Brighton	**30**

In effect then, all those above City are in fact safe, despite their proximity to the drop, because City and Luton are in the classic death or glory game. If it ends a draw, Luton will take the plunge. If the Hatters manage to win, however, it will be City sliding through the dreaded trap door. The only slight possibility comes from Birmingham City's trip to The Dell, where a four-goal defeat could then bring them into the equation.

1245 City come into the game with terrible problems. Paul Power, the club captain, was quoted in this morning's Daily Express as saying "This is the most vital game of my career". This from a man who led his side proudly down the tunnel at Wembley exactly two years ago today for the FA Cup final with Tottenham. He told Derek Potter that "A lot of careers are riding on this one game, but the future of the club is the most important thing of all." Indeed you fear for City that, if the dreadful deed does occur later today, their finances might not survive the shock of demotion to a league currently home to the likes of Cambridge United and Carlisle. All those broken promises from the board that the future was rosy will come home to roost.

1300 The two teams come into this game in slightly improving form, although City's run of results could hardly have been worse since they beat West Ham 2-0 at Maine Road on 16th April. Since then they have been tonked at Highbury 3-0, lost a critical home game to Forest 1-2 and scraped a win at fellow strugglers Brighton, to relegate the Seagulls in that dramatic game that we covered only seven days ago. If nerves were jangling at the Goldstone Ground, that was nothing compared to what they are about to go through for 90 minutes at Maine Road today. What do nerves do if they are past jangling? Any ideas to us please.

There have in fact been nerves aplenty along the way and since John Bond's shock resignation after the 0-4 FA Cup defeat at the very same Goldstone Ground in the last week of January, the results have gone from bad to worse. Here is the miserable trail since John Benson took over:

Tottenham	(h)	2-2
Coventry	(a)	0-4
Sunderland	(a)	2-3
Everton	(h)	0-0
Man United	(h)	1-2
Swansea	(a)	1-4
Southampton	(a)	1-4
Ipswich	(h)	0-1
West Brom	**(a)**	**2-0**
Liverpool	(h)	0-4
Stoke	(a)	0-1
West Ham	**(h)**	**2-0**
Arsenal	(a)	0-3
Forest	(h)	1-2
Brighton	**(a)**	**1-0**

Three wins from 15 in anyone's language is relegation form. John Benson has the unenviable task of attempting to stop the rot today and avoid going down in history as the man who took City to the second division on the back of a record like that.

Luton, meanwhile, had a stunning 5-1 home defeat to Everton to stomach and, presented with the chance to leap frog City on Monday night with their game in hand, lost at Old Trafford. United boss Ron Atkinson was, however, impressed, saying "They play the most enterprising football of all the clubs at the bottom of the table". City boss John Benson has already said that they are one of the "most courageous and attractive sides in the first division". City have been warned.

Luton have of course already beaten City once this season, on December 11th, a 3-1 victory at Kenilworth Road. This was the game, after which John Bond said he'd rather lose than draw if it meant his team had tried. Ironically today he might have looked at the situation quite differently as the latter is all City need to survive. That defeat in December left City in 10th place and Luton safe in 19th. It all looks decidedly grimmer this afternoon for both these famous clubs.

1345 First look around and the streets outside the ground are already looking very busy with the gates just opening. City's crowds are way down on last season, understandably so, and the 45,400 who turned up here for the derby defeat to United is by far the biggest of the season. Peter Swales and Bernard Halford have been drumming up support throughout the week, urging the fans to come and give the team one last push for safety. In today's Mail secretary Halford was hoping for a crowd beyond 35,000 for this one, although City's last few home games v Ipswich, Everton, West Ham and Forest have all failed to clear 25,000 and even the visit of champions-to-be Liverpool only just brought in 35,000 for a game that has seen a full house of between 48,000 and 52,000 over recent years.

1400 In case nobody was listening, here's what chairman Peter Swales and manager John Benson have had to say:

Swales -*"I won"t resign and run away. I understand the frustration of the fans because, let's face it, we have been awful."*

Benson *"There's enough pride in the dressing room to keep us up. The morale and spirit of the players could eventually save us. Though I do feel that some players have it in their heads that we won't win again".*

Fighting talk you might say, but these are quotes from the Ipswich home defeat on March 26th. Since then the pressure has only got heavier and now they all face the crunch together. You can't help thinking that this kind of desperate scrap is all pretty alien stuff for City's stars and that Luton are better adjusted to these kinds of battles. Their team is made up of players, who are familiar with life's school of hard knocks. On the other hand, City are facing something way out of their comfort zone today.

1430 Maine Road is filling up nicely and it looks like there will be a larger crowd than expected. They are filing in by their thousands to back Benson's beleaguered side one last time. The little stalls selling scarves and badges were doing a terrific trade as I came into the ground, as were the usual hot dog and burger vans parked along Claremont Road and Lloyd Street.

1435 Team news is just reaching us and it's exactly the same side for City as last week in that emotional cliff-hanger at Brighton.

CITY line up like this:

1. Alex Williams
2. Ray Ranson
3. Bobby McDonald
4. Nicky Reid
5. Kevin Bond
6. Tommy Caton
7. Dennis Tueart
8. Kevin Reeves
9. Graham Baker
10.Asa Hartford
11. Paul Power
Sub: Steve Kinsey

That will broadly work as a 4-4-2 with Bond shoring up midfield in front of young Tommy Caton and Nicky Reid, aided by Baker and Power. Tueart and Reeves pushed further forward with Hartford prompting behind them. As you can see, the names mentioned already suggest this is the kind of game that City should not be involved in.

And LUTON TOWN look like this:

1. Tony Godden
2. Kirk Stephens
3. Shaun Elliot
4. Clive Goodyear
5. Wayne Turner
6. Ricky Hill
7. Brian Horton
8. Mal Donaghy
9. Brian Stein
10.Trevor Aylott
11.Paul Walsh

Luton's sub today is Raddy Antic, a little-known David Pleat signing from Yugoslavia. The big surprise is the inclusion of top scorer Brian Stein who has apparently passed a late fitness test and will take his place alongside quicksilver Paul Walsh up front. The programme had even gone as far as to put Ray Daniel in upfront for Luton, but I can confirm Stein plays and that is a big boost for the Hatters. He has only played once in the last five months after a slow-healing foot injury. Big gamble by David Pleat, that one.

Referee today is Mr Arnold Chalinor of Rotherham. I hope he's brought his asbestos underpants, because he is going to need them. He will be helped by linesman John Kirkby from Sheffield with the red flag and Des Tweats from Poulton-le-Fylde with the orange flag. According to today's programme, the match ball has been donated by Northwest Flooring and City fans will be hoping that it is their opponents that are floored by a quarter to five this evening.

1445 It is still a quarter of an hour to kick off but the old ground is already throbbing. There's a terrific atmosphere from the Kippax and North Stands in particular, with not a single spare seat in the Platt Lane by the looks of things. Luton small band of followers, kitted out in their straw hats are to the right hand end of the Kippax and are massively outnumbered over there.

1450 Dennis Tueart, England international and star of two great spells at this club, is warming up on the pitch with one or two of his team mates. The irony for him is that he has been in a similar situation before, when playing Luton in the last game of the 1974-75 season. The game at Kenilworth Road ended one-one, Tueart scored for City and Luton were relegated. City will be hoping nobody mentions that to Luton captain Brian Horton, already a great motivator of his troops, as that will give him handy material to get the Luton players up for the task today.

The teams that day, incidentally, were: CITY: Corrigan, Hammond, Donachie, Doyle, Booth, Oakes, Hartford, Bell, Marsh, Daniels, Tueart. LUTON: Barber, John Ryan, Buckley, Anderson, Faulkner, Litt, Jim Ryan, Husband, Alston, West, Aston. Only Tueart and team mate Asa Hartford remain from that black day for Luton and they have both had spells away from City in the meantime (Tueart at New York Cosmos, Hartford at Everton and Forest, of course).

1455 Some rumours that the game might not kick off on time at 3pm, as the crush to get in is increasing now. Have just seen Jimmy Frizzell go by, the ex-Oldham manager now scouting for Luton, and he looked as tense as we all feel. Harry Haslam, the jovial ex-general manager could not manage a smile either, whilst comic Eddie Large, who will take his place on the City bench, was trying to fire a few quips to lighten the mood. Few takers for Eddie's humour today I'm afraid.

1458 City players are out on the pitch to a thunderous reception. A sea of hands on the Kippax over to the far side greets Paul Power as he leads the side out on his 250th appearance for the Blues. Coming out behind him is keeper Alex Williams (what a big day it is for the youngster), followed by the bushy hair of Tommy Caton and then midfielder Graham Baker. The old ground is really throbbing now. Luton fans – and there are quite a few shoehorned in now -- waving their straw hats and a giant teddy bear but their singing is being totally drowned out by the noise cascading down off the Kippax. Even the normally sedate Main Stand is on its feet today. 17 years of uninterrupted first division action is hanging in the balance here. Kick-off is only a few seconds away, as the two managers offer each other a nervous-looking handshake.

01:00 Trevor Aylott and Brian Stein get us started. City immediately into action in a raw and noisy atmosphere, with Asa Hartford quick into the tackle and feeding Ray Ranson who charges down the right touchline and swings a cross in. Held by on-loan keeper Tony Godden with Reeves and Tueart challenging immediately. You get the distinct impression it's going to be a busy afternoon for the Luton man.

04:00 Graham Baker now making inroads down the right, but Mal Donaghy rushes in to dispossess the City man. An all-action start, as widely predicted. Ball is a hot potato, though.

05:00 Kevin Bond down on the turf after seemingly taking a blow to his face from Kirk Stephens as the two challenged for a lofted ball. Bobby McDonald has also just delivered a crunching early reducer on the lively Trevor Aylott, who City will well remember for scoring the Barnsley goal that knocked them out of the League Cup in that bear pit atmosphere at Oakwell last season. Stein also moving gingerly after bumping into the – what shall we call him -- *tenacious* City full back.

09:00 First real danger from Luton. Stein rounds Nicky Reid down on the touchline and strikes a high ball in towards Mal Donaghy, who really goes for it. The Luton man makes contact but only manages a soft header, which is gathered in easily by Williams.

12:00 McDonald's cruncher on Aylott releases Power down the inside left channel but when the ball comes in to Kevin Reeves on the edge of the box, he is easily dispossessed as the ball gets tangled between his feet. A little too hasty again from City there.

16:00 Ding dong First hearing of Helen's bell as Goodyear reacts angrily to a challenge from Tueart, diving in vigorously in search of the ball on that frenzied area of the Luton box.

Mr Challinor having difficulty keeping the lid on this one in a real pressure cooker atmosphere. Fussy officiating so far from him is tending to break up the flow a little. That and the tackles flying in, of course!

18:00 Kevin Reeves sweeps the ball wide to the right to Tueart, whose quick cross is turned behind for a corner, which is cleared by the massive bulk of Paul Elliot, soaring above Kevin Bond to blot out the danger.

SO CLOSE Luton immediately sweep up to the other end, with Aylott winning a corner for the Hatters off Bobby McDonald. Horton's low effort is cleared by Caton at a stretch, but as the ball is swung back in again, Aylott traps and turns, bringing a superb flying save from Williams to tip it just over the bar. Real danger from Luton this time.

20:00 We have reached the twenty minute mark and that effort by Aylott moments ago was the first clear sign of danger so far. Luton beginning to look lively in sharp Manchester sun now. The surface is already cutting up though, especially around the centre circle, owing to the heavy rain we had here this morning.

25:00 A flying fist from Williams clears the ball above Aylott's head. Paul Power and Mal Donaghy are the latest to be down on the floor after what looked like a clash of heads. Power is getting up slowly but limping now so maybe it wasn't his head at all. Pitch is continuing to cut up quite badly in the middle.

30:00 Luton back on the attack with Caton just beating Trevor Aylott to Kirk Stephens' dangerous left wing cross.

Real chances thin on the ground still, but you can cut the atmosphere with a knife.

32:00 Luton pressure mounting Hill and Horton threatening now. Hill's cheeky lob is dealt with by McDonald whilst Horton hits one into the near post, where Stein launches himself to head narrowly wide.

42:00 City are responding to Luton's attacking with wave after wave of their own now. Reeves, blocked by Goodyear on the left, just failed to make something of Nicky Reid's deep ball across the box. Big diagonal ball from Bond had set Tueart free, great pass from the big defender. Real noise now from the City fans, as they sense their side beginning to turn the screw.

45:00 Getting closer Right on half time danger for Luton, as Kevin Reeves strokes a right foot shot across goal and just past the far post with Godden struggling. It was Nicky Reid's quick thinking that had put Reeves through down the right channel.

45:00+1 HT at Maine Road and it's goalless in the relegation dogfight:

MANCHESTER CITY 0-0 LUTON TOWN

"Maine Road will die as a force in football unless there is a shake-up," says John Bond. The former manager is getting the boot in whilst the teams chew nervously on their oranges somewhere below us.

Pick of the half times elsewhere is the stalemate between Southampton and Birmingham at The Dell, which means it looks increasingly unlikely that either side in this match can rely on that game to throw up a lifeline. Meanwhile champions Liverpool are losing at Vicarage Road to 2nd placed Watford, Villa lead Arsenal and Manchester United are being held at Notts County. Tottenham are heading for the UEFA Cup with a 2-0 half time lead over Stoke.

Half time analysis: Much too much hanging on this game for it to produce aeven a modicum of decent coordinated football. It's invigorating, watchable fare, but only because of the giant trapdoor swinging open below these two sides. Luton have settled well and look frisky in attack, with plenty of ball coming through right back Stephens. City on the other hand look very nervous, have given away a lot of possession in midfield and will be looking to the likes of Hartford and Power, the midfield men with big game experience, to settle things down a little and get their passing game going in the second period. You get the feeling the longer this game foes on goalless, the more likely a single slip up will be costly.

46:00 Second half underway at Maine Road. The sun is still out as Kevin Reeves and Dennis Tueart get us up and running again. No changes to either side at half time, as Graham Baker knocks a long ball straight through to Tony Godden. Early feel in the second half for the busier of the two keepers so far.

A reminder that City have conceded a total of 69 goals in their slide down the table, whereas Luton's defence has been much more porous with 84 goals flying into the back of their net so far. Could it be that just the one will make the difference today?

56: 10 Big chance for Luton Town! Kirk Stephens quickly into action down the right, as his cross cannons off Bond for a corner to Luton. Donaghy climbs above Bond at the corner and it's Paul Walsh with a firm shot past the sprawling Bobby McDonald blocked by Alex Williams *in extremis*. Williams produces a fantastic reflex save with his legs in an unsighted position. That was close for City and the crowd is getting pretty jittery. Even Helen's bell has gone quiet now. First round of Come on You Hatters can be heard above the general hubbub.

True to their attacking philosophy, Luton are continuing with three up front here and only the three in midfield, Hill, Horton and the more defensively minded Donaghy. It's a bold move, but will it be their undoing? If it goes wrong, they're down, don't forget.

60:15 Movement down on the two benches, but of a very different kind. Luton boss David Pleat has substitute Raddy Antic warming up already. As if he didn't have enough forwards out there already, but Luton do need a goal of course. If it stays like this City are safe. As a result the only City activity is Eddie Large swapping places with the returning City physio Roy Bailey down on the touchline. Roy either refilling his bucket or the nerves are getting to him in another way.

62:00 Asa Hartford desperately trying to galvanise City in midfield. The little Scotsman is everywhere, biting into the tackles and delivering forward balls. Has to be said that there's a muted response around him though and City need Baker and Power to get some more passes fed to the forwards, who are just not receiving any chances. Dennis Tueart and Kevin Reeves will get you goals if you can get them through into shooting positions.

64:00 First substitution: Antic > Turner: Raddy Antic is indeed coming on and it will be the tree trunk legs of Wayne Turner that the Yugoslav replaces. He's also a midfielder but an attacking one, so Pleat is winding up the pressure on City. It's a bold move but it's bound to leave some holes at the back. Can City respond? Turner hobbles off and gets his cheeks slapped enthusiastically by his manager as he puts his tracksuit top on. Game on.

69:00 McDonald close Storming run from Nicky Reid, feeds Power on the left in front of a sunlit Kippax, comes deep to Baker, who wins a free kick. Lofted in by Hartford for the bushy-haired head of Tommy Caton, who glances it goalwards. Bobby

McDonald is a whisker away as Godden claws at fresh air. That's woken up the home crowd again. Real noise around the old ground again now, as City up the ante.

70:00 Legs everywhere From the resulting corner, Tueart's effort is smothered. Desperate stuff from a now overworked Tony Godden, resulting in a third corner in a row. City getting very close now. Godden, not the tallest of goalkeepers, is certainly earning his crust from his new employers this afternoon.

71:00 PANIC Third corner comes flying in from Asa Hartford, Godden's out again and there's utter panic in the Luton box, but referee Challinor has blown for an infringement. Wow, things are hotting up now and the crowd is coming nicely to the boil. Not sure Tony Godden anticipated his season ending like this when he signed on loan from West Brom in March to cover for the injured Jake Findlay. One way or another, he's going to remember today for the rest of his life.

72:15 It might be hectic out there. It might be the most critical cut and thrust of the entire season for these two sides and their poor drained fans, but Luton physio John Sheridan has just lit his pipe down in the away dugout. I kid you not. The coolest man in the entire place and that includes me. He is also wearing a red tracksuit jacket, which is a little provocative considering where we are. No pipe for Eddie Large in the home dugout, but John Benson and Tony Book sure like they need a funny story telling to them. Grim faces all the way.

75:00 LUTON HIT THE BAR! Or in fact Nicky Reid hits the bar. His own bar! What drama here. Oh my word. Long shot was from Kirk Stephens, the full back, who is having a storming game for Luton. Alex Williams was down very well to parry it, but he couldn't hold onto it in the melée and it cannoned back off Nicky Reid's shins and smacked the top of the cross bar to go for a corner. What a close scrape for City. Poor Reid looks like he's seen the Ghost of Christmas Past or maybe it was the Relegation Spectre floating in front of the young defender's eyes.

77:00 Its Stephens again, with a speculative cross that Brian Stein just misses. Wobbly moments now for City with under a quarter of an hour to go. Luton have to score and they're doing their utmost to do just that. City hanging on a bit at the moment.

Just to remind you that Kirk Stephens was a £5,000 David Pleat buy from Nuneaton Borough. A real bargain he looks this afternoon.

78:00 Raddy Antic taking Luton's corners now. This one's too deep, flying over the crowded box and bringing out Helen's bell once again. Can a bell sound relieved? This one sure does.

79:00 SO CLOSE CITY Now it's City turning the screw as Asa Hartford embarks on a terrific run cutting inside from the right wing that takes him right along the edge of the box, jinking past one, two, three defenders before back heeling it into the path of Paul Power, whose cross is met by Tueart's header and cleared. Great move by City. Terrific run from Hartford.

84:00 About six minutes to go here and the tension is utterly unbearable. There are fans in the Main Stand who are having difficulty watching this now. Ranson clears for a Luton corner, Donaghy gets his head on it but Caton is there and it's another corner. Desperate, desperate stuff. Luton trying all they know, City bodies blocking everything they can. Reeves scrambles the ensuing corner away. Everyone was up for Luton, leaving them very open to a counter, if City can gather themselves. Luton Town, as we stand, some five minutes or so away from the drop.

85:00 Caton clatters into Ricky Hill. Exactly five minutes to go. Nerves on a knife edge now.

86:20 GOAL!!! LUTON TOWN! UNBELIEVABLE!! WITH JUST FOUR MINUTES TO GO. Oh my oh my. **LUTON HAVE SCORED** and in the most nerve-jangling of situations. Aylott winning possession in midfield, so many bodies in there, he manages to get it out to Brian Stein on the right who delivers a loopy cross inviting Williams to gather, but the keeper cannot reach the outswinger as Kevin Bond is in the way and only punches weakly to Raddy Antic on the edge of the box. His first time shot back in is touched by Williams and the deflection off the keeper's hands takes the ball just wide of the man on the line and into the net. **What absolute, nerve-shredding, red blooded drama here at Maine Road. The place is in an absolute tumult and City have next to no time to save their skins now. The players are looking at each other as if someone has just told them a tidal wave is coming. Wide eyed expressions of panic everywhere.**

It's all hands on deck for City, who look utterly shell-shocked. Steve Kinsey straight on for a disappointing Graham Baker and the ball is being lumped forward any which way. Man in the crowd in front of me is almost literally pulling his hair out. Scenes of great discomfort amongst the faithful here.

89:00 Godden down to smother Hartford's ball, as the Kippax gathers itself for one last lung-busting call to arms. Hearty rendition of We'll Support You Ever More sounds like they think it's curtains to me though.

90:00 Time nearly up. Just what Mr Challinor wants to add on now and there have been precious few injuries, despite the red blooded nature of the contest. Stephens whacks it high into touch. Luton just banging it anywhere now.

90:00+1 CORNER TO CITY Godden misses Reid's high cross and it goes for a corner. Hartford whacks it in quickly and there's an almighty struggle with McDonald laying it to Kinsey whose shot smacks into the goalkeeper's chest, but the referee has blown for a push by McDonald. This is desperate stuff for City.

90:00+2 GAME OVER: LUTON HAVE SAVED THEMSELVES. CITY ARE RELEGATED FOR THE FIRST TIME IN 17 YEARS!!!! The ref's whistle goes with Dennis Tueart on the ball, a poignant one as it may well now be his last ever touch in a Manchester City shirt. **Luton Town have done it, surviving in the most incredible manner possible here. What drama.** David Pleat is galloping across the Maine Road turf like a man gone mental, clasping his fawn suit at the front as he gambols across the Maine Road turf and he's making a bee-line for his captain Brain Horton, who has been absolutely magnificent. There are police horses on the field too and fans streaming on from the Kippax side and Platt Lane ends. Let's hope this doesn't get nasty, as the Luton players have gone right over to the far side to salute their fans in the corner.

Indeed it is getting a bit hectic out there. Some punches thrown at Ricky Hill and Brian Stein by an irate mob now on the pitch. Police are trying to clear the field whilst the players leave, Luton players running off jubilant. Most of City's players have disappeared down the tunnel already but I can still make out Dennis Tueart trudging off head bowed with supporters consoling him. Horton tried to shake his hand but Tueart just shrugged it away. The City man is inconsolable. Hartford is there too. The old guard reluctant to leave the pitch for obvious reasons. Nobody tried to lift his side more than Asa Hartford today but it was not to be. **City drop to the second division.**

So, this fine club with all of its traditions goes down to the second division in the most heart-rending of circumstances. You have to feel sorry for Tony Book and John Benson and those fans that have stuck with them as the season fell apart. Nobody deserves to be put through the wringer like that. But, it's Luton who will be playing first division football next season and we must congratulate them on a terrifically brave display here today as we wave farewell to City and hope they can do what Tottenham, Manchester United and Nottingham Forest have all done in the last 17 years and that's come back from relegation and prove that it doesn't need to be the end of the story, but can just as easily be the springboard to a brave new world.

We'll have some quotes for you just as soon as the pitch is cleared and we can access some extremely jubilant players on the one hand and very disconsolate ones on the other.

Meantime, today's crowd has been confirmed at 42,843, City's second highest of this dreadful season and a good few of them are still on the pitch now as we have the slightly unedifying sight of police on horseback on the Maine Road pitch right now.

City chairman is the first to make himself available to talk to us: "As the head of the club I have always said that the buck stops with me. But all my directors have come to me and told me not to pack it in – and I hadn't thought of it anyway. This is the saddest day of my life but I won't put my head in the gas oven."

Well indeed, no need for that, Mr Swales, but good news for City fans that the chairman looks to be of the intention of staying to organise the restucuring of this great club fallen on hard times.

Young Tommy Caton is in the tunnel: "If there weren't so many people about I would be crying. It's the worst moment of my life."

Ricky Hill is explaining what happened on the pitch at the end: "Some City fans got onto the pitch where we were celebrating with the manager and the fans. Obviously they weren't very happy. I got hit a couple of times, one in the face one on the back of the head, but I'm happy!"

Well quite. Here's a less happy man, Tony Book, who has seen a few triumphs in his time at the club and now tastes the bitterness of disaster: "It's very sad to see a dressing room like the one I've just been in. It kills me really. Now we have got to be brave, got to be strong and bounce straight back."

No sign of John Benson as yet. It will be interesting to see how far into the summer he lasts. Early money is on Monday morning.

The disaster course of a sunken ship: most supporters agree that the rot set in when Peter Swales brought Malcolm Allison back in for a second stint at Maine Road. Successful manager Tony Book was pushed to one side to make way for Swales' glamour boy. Allison took no time at all in dismantling Book's trophy winning side, discharging the likes of Dave Watson, Peter Barnes, Gary Owen, Brian Kidd, Joe Royle, Mike Channon et al.

He replaced them with youngsters, trialists and over-hyped signings from lower leagues. Michael Robinson, Bobby Shinton and Steve Daley. Money was leeching from every crevice. Bad buy upon bad buy heaped pressure on City's finances until they had to start cutting their cloth to suit the day. John Bond came in and pulled the ragged strings together for a while, turning City into a Cup Final side in 1981 but trouble was mounting off the pitch. Interest rates had hit 20% and City were sinking in debt. Economy became an obsession and the playing staff was pared to the bone. City scoured the free transfer market. Bond left in a huff but City were happy to promote the under-qualified Benson from within. It saved another wage, nothing more.

And now this.

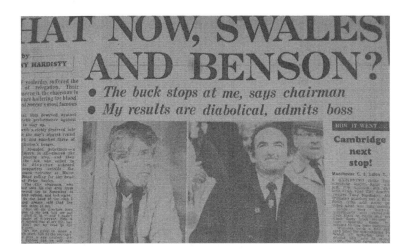

Saturday 7th November 1987
Division Two. Manchester City v Huddersfield Town

"It's White. The tenth is there for the taking. It's going to be a hat trick for David White. And ten for Manchester City!!"

Welcome to a mean, cold and damp Manchester, where City entertain bottom club Huddersfield Town in a second division fixture with little to appeal to fans of either club. It's 10th v 22nd under a blanket grey sky at Maine Road this afternoon and, if you've made the effort to get out and travel to this one, you surely will be rewarded in heaven.

Bovril sales will be high today. As the temperatures sink towards freezing, it's an excuse to show your colours at least with a tightly wrapped scarf to keep the inclement elements at bay.

City's home crowds have been dwindling rapidly this season. 15,000 v Millwall, 16,000 v Leicester and 17,000 v Barnsley all tell their own tale of a club that is beginning to lose its way. This is after all City's third season of 2nd division football this decade and there are good prospects of a fourth next year. Chairman Peter Swales has issued the usual optimistic statements, but it is clear that if City remain marooned in this kind of obscurity for long, folk will begin to worry for their prospects and if those loyal fans are beginning to stop coming, things must be getting serious.

There is good news and bad news for City management duo Mel Machin and Jimmy Frizzell. The club arrives at this fixture on a five game unbeaten run, which has included a dramatic 4-2 win away at leaders Bradford City and a tremendous display in the Littlewoods Cup to dispose of Brian Clough's Nottingham Forest 3-0. So, the goals are going in, confidence is rising and this team of mainly local youngsters is beginning to show signs that it possesses what it takes to get the club back to the top.

The bad news comes in the form of injuries to front-men Imre Varadi, who will miss this one after scoring four in the afore-mentioned five-game run, and long-term absentee Paul Moulden, who is still recovering from a broken leg. That leaves City with just Paul Stewart and newcomer Tony Adcock to fill the front places. Adcock has managed just three appearances and one goal since his arrival from Colchester United in the summer, but he is likely to start today alongside ex-Blackpool man Stewart.

1400 We don't have the team news yet, but it looks like youngster Paul Lake is set to play, possibly in place of fellow youth team graduate Ian Brightwell. In the opposition ranks today will be Andy May, ex-City midfield man, who has been doing a good job in Huddersfield's middle ranks in what has been a seriously complicated season for the Tykes so far. Malcolm Macdonald is the fresh new manager, less than a month into his appointment as Steve Smith's successor after the latter resigned from his post. The ex-Newcastle and Arsenal hit-man was within a point of taking Fulham up to the first division in his previous job at Craven Cottage and is likely to try to turn the Terriers into a more attacking side in light of his own goal-strewn career. Already they have passed the landmark of notching their first win of the season, however belated that may have been, a week ago against Millwall at Leeds Road, so things are beginning to lighten in West Yorkshire too.

1410 Well, Granada's outside broadcast unit begs to differ with our opinion of the status of this game. The television trucks are parked outside the Main Stand and the game will be on

Granada TV tomorrow afternoon. I admire their optimism and bow to their superior knowledge of all things football. Commentator Martin Tyler has just passed our position carrying his wad of notes and we have also spotted Elton Welsby, The Man in the Tie. Let's hope they're right about this one and I'm wrong.

1415 Team news is in as the rain tumbles down on to the verdant Maine Road pitch. The ground staff are out forking it over, with Stan Gibson pointing and arranging right up to the last minutes before kick-off.

Paul Lake indeed comes in for Brightwell, who he replaced as a second half substitute in City's last outing, a 1-1 draw with Middlesbrough and – as expected - Tony Adcock starts too, so City look like this:

Nixon: Gidman, Hinchcliffe, Clements, Redmond; Lake, White, McNab, Simpson; Adcock, Stewart. Sub today is Ian Brightwell, who as we said loses his place to Paul Lake.

We'll have the Huddersfield line-up just as soon as it comes in.

1430 Huddersfield boss Macdonald has just walked past us and gave us a few quick words. He seemed happy and positive after the win over Millwall last week. "Play like that will certainly get us out of trouble," he told us. "We are looking forward to this game instead of being apprehensive about it," he added. His team news is as follows:
Cox: Brown, Bray, Banks, Webster, Walford, Barham, May, Shearer; Winter, Cork.

Ex-Norwich flier and twice England international Mark Barham starts and they are buoyed at the back by experienced ex-Arsenal man Steve Walford, as well as ex-City midfielder May, who also plays. Danger men are perhaps going to be midfield powerhouse Ian Banks, a £40,000 buy from Leicester and voted into the PFA 2nd division team of the year in 81-82 when playing for Barnsley, and striker Duncan Shearer, for whom Macdonald has already turned down bids from Leeds and Aberdeen in recent weeks. He is Town's top scorer.

Referee today is Mr Robbie Hart from Darlington, a late replacement for George Tyson, who is unwell. Mr Nuttall of Mansfield will wave the red trim flag and Mr Taylor of Shipley will take charge of the yellow trimmed flag and also wave it about occasionally.

1445 Smallish crowd gathering in the gloom on the Kippax across the way. Can see plenty of gaps in the terraces and it's always a sign when the crush barriers are still visible with only 15 minutes to kick-off. The rain is still coming down steadily and the sky over Rusholme is heavy and darkening. Looks like there might be a deluge a little later.

A win today could take City above Millwall and Swindon into 8th, while, if the points head east across the Pennines tonight, Town will still be rooted to the bottom, thanks to the five point difference to Reading in 21st.

Ripple of applause as the stadium announcer crackles into half-hearted life here. Sounds a bit like City are employing Norman Collier to make the announcements this afternoon, as the feed keeps cutting out. No help either from the electric scoreboard at the back of the North Stand, which is sending out a message in something approaching Cyrillic script. Another job for Mr Swales to get his teeth into there.

1459 Out come the teams to a muted reception. A small knot of some three hundred or so Huddersfield fans are at the very front of the Platt Lane, dwarfed by a stand that contains some 8,000 seats. There is a section of standing supporters too away on the uncovered end of the Kippax. They will watch their side play in yellow shirts with black checks today. Painful on the yes but showing up gloriously against the green of the pitch and the cavernous black of the Kippax behind them.

1500 KICK OFF is on time and we are away here. Huddersfield launch us into the game, take three steps into City's half and fall over, ceding possession immediately to the home side. I hope that isn't an omen. The ball is back with Eric Nixon.

1501 Early touch for Andy May, the ex-City man, who looks right up for this one. Buzzing around the midfield in these opening seconds.

1503 Good early signs here. Huddersfield probing eagerly through Ian Banks and Julian Winter. McNab and Stewart showing early for City. Some brisk early exchanges with the away side coming out on top. Through ball from Cork is swept up capably by Kenny Clements and deposited with 'keeper Nixon once again.

1504 CHANCE! First effort on goal and it's the visitors who are cranking up the early pressure. First corner of the game, off David White, raises distant cheers of "yellows, yellows" from the other end of the ground. Corner is swung over, headed clear by David White and smashed high over the bar by the over-eager Julian Winter.

1505 CLOSE AGAIN Dominic Cork is in behind Steve Redmond and is inches wide of Nixon's far post. Bright start by Macdonald's men, with May and Winter dominating McNab and Lake so far. City, with two wide midfielders in White and Paul Simpson, need more bodies in the middle, where they are being outnumbered and outmanoeuvred.

1511 First City chance falls to new man Adcock, who tries a back-heel in a crowded box from Paul Stewart's feed, but it strikes Malcolm Brown and is cleared. With over 350 first team games for the Terriers, Brown certainly knows how to handle himself and will be a major obstacle for the somewhat green Adcock to deal with.

1513 GOAL TO CITY. MANCHESTER CITY 1 HUDDERSFIELD 0 I spoke too soon evidently. In the very next bit of action, Neil McNab picks up a loose ball and runs across the Huddersfield defence, including the back-pedalling Mr Brown, who stands off him long enough to allow the Scotsman a sight of goal. McNab needs no more encouragement than that and shoots left footed low past Cox's left hand post. Against the run of play, it must be said, City are in the lead here.

1514 City in the mood now. They win the ball straight back from the kick off with John Gidman launching an audacious ball down the right touchline, setting White free in space. The cross is cleared, but City come straight back with Stewart feeding Paul Lake. His shot ricochets free for a corner.

Huddersfield suddenly under serious pressure having conceded.

1517 Dominic Cork so close to an equaliser for the visitors. Mark Barham's cross comes flying in from the right touchline, Cork chests it down expertly and just as he's about to pull the trigger, Kenny Clements stretches out a leg and pokes the ball back to Eric Nixon. Close call for City.

1528 It's Huddersfield pressing for the equaliser again as Cork sets up Shearer with a neat reverse ball in the box but the 11-goal striker screws his shot harmlessly wide. Sighs of relief in the North Stand. Huddersfield determined to make a game of this one.

1529 GOAL!!! CITY! MANCHESTER CITY 2 HUDDERSFIELD 0 Paul Stewart makes it two! Adcock slides Stewart in down the right channel in front of the Main Stand. The striker takes two strides, one touch and buries it past Cox's far post. No chance for the big keeper and an enhanced reputation for this potent goal scorer Stewart. Difficult to shrug off the ball, direct, forceful and a nose for goal. What a bargain he's proving to be. As for Huddersfield, every time they show some signs of life, City go straight ahead and extinguish all hope.

1534 GOAL. CITY! MANCHESTER CITY 3 HUDDERSFIELD 0
West Yorkshire hope just disappeared altogether. It's raining goals at Maine Road now. Just as the visitors were getting a bit of a foothold, City slam the door shut on them. And it's Tony Adcock with his 100th career goal. Made this time by Paul Stewart and Andy Hinchcliffe out on the left, the latter's

cross inch perfect into a big space in the middle of the box, where Adcock had time to run onto it and plant a header through Cox's flailing arms right into the centre of the goal. Greet ball in by the left back.

1536 Identical break, different outcome. This time it's Paul Simpson down the left with a pulverising run and cross. Adcock has a copy of his previous header two minutes ago, but it's softer this time and Cox dives to his right, holding onto it, as Stewart is waiting for any scraps. Town fans behind the goal are clapping deliriously that he held onto something.

1541 GOAL CITY!! It didn't last long. **MANCHESTER CITY 4 HUDDERSFIELD 0** Again City prospering down the left side in front of the Kippax. Simpson slid through by Paul Lake's pass, hammers down the touchline, has to cut back inside, then doubles back and goes wide again, to get a cross in right on the touchline. It's squared to David White, completely unmarked, but still needing some deft footwork to swivel and flick it in close-range with one movement. City suddenly well on top. Huddersfield must be asking what they did wrong.

A sudden and dramatic blitz from the Blues has coincided with a sudden drop-off in intensity from Huddersfield and they find themselves 4-0 down. This has been quite an extraordinary first half. Huddersfield starting better, carving out the first chance and playing their part right up to the third goal, but they have been clinically picked off by this young City side.

1542 Tony Adcock, amazingly, finds himself straight through on the keeper again, but his attempt to chip Cox goes all wrong and the ball soars high and wide. The red-haired ex-Colchester man looks forlornly at the turf, as if blaming a loose divot. Who knows what made him place it over there.

1545 HALF TIME Nixon grabs the ball at the back post before Andy May can connect with Barham's cross and it's all done for this half. Extraordinary stuff from City. Malcolm Macdonald hurries away down the tunnel. He will have some interesting things to tell his players during the half time break. Having been attacked from the off, City can thank their experienced spine of Gidman, Clements and McNab for holding them together and their immaculate front-man Stewart for leading the counter-charge.

Huddersfield will want to tighten up in the second half, it goes without saying, but with their second game of the season in mind, when they were thrashed 1-6 at Plymouth Argyle, they will be doing everything they can to avoid emulating that particular score-line. They have looked able in attack with Cork showing up well alongside Shearer but the experienced Brown and Walford at the back have looked one-paced and pedestrian when faced with the fire, speed and spirit of Simpson, White and Stewart.

Start of 2nd half - MANCHESTER CITY 4 HUDDERSFIELD 0

1601 City start the second period attacking – and that really is the word for what they're doing this afternoon – the North Stand goal, where Brian Cox is busily slapping his gloves together in anticipation of some more work. It's a scrappy, bitty start to the second half so far though.

1604 CLOSE It's Huddersfield quickest out of the blocks, winning the first corner of the 2nd half. Andy Hinchcliffe is forced to head behind and as the corner comes in, Duncan Shearer's header is goal-bound until John Gidman pops up to head the ball off the line from right under the crossbar. Town starting with a rush, but then they did that in the first half too. Only four goals to claw back.

1608 GOAL. CITY 5-UP! Well now it's five they have to claw back and it would seem the mini revival has been squashed before it could even call itself such a thing. This was simplicity itself. Gidman, having saved the day in his own box just a couple of minutes ago, strikes a long ball through to Paul Simpson on the left wing. Simpson takes it on a pace or two then cracks a deep cross that evades everyone and leaves Cox in no man's land. It bounces high but Tony Adcock slashes a fierce shot back across the keeper and into the far top corner. What a lovely finish from Adcock, who is now on a hat trick.

1609 NEARLY SIX! City threatening to run riot here as Huddersfield begin to collapse like a partially cooked soufflé. Paul Stewart it is that surges through the defence, evading tackle after tackle. He passes it left to Simpson whose snap shot is saved desperately by Cox, the man with the warmest gloves in football this afternoon.

1622 AND NOW IT IS SIX After a couple more missed half chances, City hit the sixth. Incredible scenes here. It's Simpson once again providing down the left. Simple, long cross to the back post where Stewart rises above the crowd to nod back across Cox with his marker Malcolm Brown flapping wildly to get into position. It's Stewart's 10th of the season and he, quite remarkably, is also now on for his hat trick. **Manchester City 6 Huddersfield Town 0**

1623 UNBELIEVABLE: IT'S SEVEN!!! City have gone berserk. The Kippax in full throated joy now, as the visitors are getting an embarrassing mauling here. A minute has passed since the sixth goal. This time the fault is totally Simon Webster's. The defender dallies on the ball and is robbed by Tony Adcock on the near touchline, who speeds towards Cox, waits for him to commit himself and dinks it past him low into the near side of the goal. Three for Adcock, seven for City. What a game this is turning out to be. **Manchester City 7 (SEVEN) Huddersfield Town 0** I've been waiting a long time to do the spelling-the-big-score-line-thing. Today City are making it happen.

A fantastic hat trick by Tony Adcock, whose chances have been few and far between since joining the club. He's more than making up for it today.

1624 Inches away from eight! Another coruscating run from the unplayable Stewart down the right forces yet another corner, which ends up at the feet of the same player. This time he misses badly to the right of the goal when very well placed. That could have given us two hat trick men in one game.

1627 Now it's Steve Redmond having a pot-shot. I think all the City players think this might be their day, the way this game is unfolding. Stewart again winning a corner, Lake's header on, Redmond mashes it high and handsome.

1637 WE HAVE TWO HAT TRICK HEROES AT MAINE ROAD! Paul Stewart grabs his third in emphatic fashion and it's eight-nil City! Where will all this end? The Huddersfield players now look completely shell-shocked. They are just waiting either for the ground to swallow them up or the referee to put them out of their misery, whichever comes first.

Again the goal is simplicity itself. A Huddersfield attack breaks down, Adcock feeds Hinchcliffe through down the left with a perfect defence splitting pass, the left back advances and slots a low ball to the far post, where Stewart only has to maintain his stride and stroke it into the net. You'll never guess what the Kippax is now chanting?! Some people are never satisfied. "We want nine!" reverberates around the old ground and I can guarantee that's the first time anyone in here today has heard that one sung at the football.

"All we are saying is give us a goal...." Easy to be in a good mood now, City fans!

1640 Dying embers of the game now. The visitors look like the boxer, whose team forgot to throw in the towel.

1641 AND IT'S A KNOCK OUT! NINE FOR CITY! Never ever seen anything like this. Quite incredibly, it's now NINE-NIL to Manchester City and the teleprinter on Grandstand will have to spell out the score in letters just like I am doing. I can just hear David Coleman's voice now. He will also want to know how it happened: Adcock again involved in the build-up (since he clinched his own threesome, he has been busy setting up everyone else). His cross hit the outstretched heel of Steve Walford, who I had forgotten was still on the pitch, falling beautifully for David White to smack home with his right foot. Incredibly, although we have practically run out of time now, White is now also one goal away from a hat trick of his own.

A quick look at the record books tells us we are now in record breaking territory. City's only visits to the world of double figures were last century against Lincoln City (11-3) and Darwen (10-0). Well they've got nine today and it has been a pleasure and a privilege to be present on such an occasion.

1643 FEISTY John Gidman is certainly not taking it easy. With the crowd baying for ten, it's all getting a bit ragged. Gidman has just elbowed Ian Gray in the face and instead of taking his ticking off with a bowed head and a grin, the experienced Gidman is arguing the point for all his worth. You'd think we were approaching the 90th minute at 0-0 here.

Last chance for City to grab total glory, as Steve Redmond again appears in the box for a corner, but his header lacks power and is easily saved (there's a first for today) by Brian Cox, who incredibly is still out there keeping goal for Huddersfield Town.

1644 PENALTY!
.... TO HUDDERSFIELD!!!! Gidman again with his temperament askew, has brought down Dominik Cork in the box. City's last chance of getting ten has certainly evaporated thanks to Gidman's hot head.

1645 GOAL TO HUDDERSFIELD. ANDY MAY. Of all people to stop the rot, it's Hudderfield's one and only ex-City player Andy May, who calmly strokes the ball high past Eric Nixon. He looks pleased with himself but the smile is a wry one from May. **MANCHESTER CITY 9 HUDDERSFIELD TOWN 1**

1646 OH MY GOD. THEY HAVE ONLY GONE AND DONE IT. A MINUTE INTO INJURY TIME IT IS TEN AT MAINE ROAD. A HISTORICAL DAY, A HISTORICAL MOMENT AND IT'S THREE HAT TRICKS ON TOP OF EVERYTHING ELSE. David White grabs the glory, one on one with the humiliated Brian Cox, he skips past him, heads a little wide, but smacks it unerringly past Webster on the line. The roof is coming off here in the gloom and darkness of a grim Manchester evening, which Manchester City have completely and utterly lit up with their sparkling football. Ten-one to City!

FULL TIME at Maine Road. City have edged this one 10-1.

Paul Stewart and Tony Adcock are down on the pitch arms around each other with a gaggle of photographers surrounding them. These, ladies and gentlemen, will be the images adorning your Sunday papers tomorrow and the Pink Final after five o'clock. Not sure where David White is among the throng of well wishers but I'm sure they'll be reunited shortly. Brian Cox trudges past with his head bowed low. Malcolm Macdonald has stayed to shake a few hands, but I'm sure he'll be keen to leave the City players and staff to soak up the applause and get back to the sanctuary of the dressing room. What an afternoon we have been treated to here.

Last, quick word from Paul Stewart, whose time is highly desired at the moment by the men of the press. "It's great to be part of such a historical moment," he says in an understated voice. The rest of us will be left to do the hysterical stuff later on. Here is City's man of the match with his feet well and truly on the floor.

I for one would like to know who gets the match ball in what is a unique situation here. I have just seen groundsman Stan Gibson scurrying past with one of those great net nags full of Mitre Deltas, so maybe the solution is closer than we thought.

Here's a remarkably composed-looking Jimmy Frizzell: "Often in the past, playing against a team from the lower reaches of the league has been difficult and we've struggled. That could have been the case here, but we've seen an astonishing performance and a score line that has had everybody looking into the record books."

Manchester City 5 Manchester United 1
23rd September 1989.

"It's a Maine Road massacre!"

1:30 pm. Hello and welcome to Maine Road, which today hosts the 111th Manchester derby, and there will be frayed nerves on both sides, as Alex Ferguson's side travel to their cross-city rivals, managed by Mel Machin and struggling somewhat having been promoted to the top flight last season.

Because of City's recent struggles, this is the first time the two sides have met at Maine Road for three years, for what should be a fascinating match. United will be firm favourites, but form often goes out the window for a derby, and neither side has hit the heights this season.

Still, a nice day in Manchester as the teams warm up out on the pitch.

1:45 pm. So City have had a mixed run as a promoted team after two seasons out of the top flight, which is not that surprising. They came up in 2nd place last season, behind runaway leaders Chelsea and ahead of Steve Coppell's stylish Crystal Palace side. That 1-1 draw at Bradford City to seal promotion is still fresh in many minds, though the result didn't matter in the end. The question over the summer was whether City could consolidate in the top division, on a tight budget. The evidence so far is not promising, though the capture of Clive Allen and also Ian Bishop in the summer has brought greater confidence to the City camp. City have nevertheless struggled, and come into today's game as underdogs. A solitary win against Queens Park Rangers is their only victory to date in six attempts, thanks to the aforementioned Allen. Just 4 points from 6 games means they are looking up the table enviously, and defeat last week whilst United were busy thrashing Millwall won't help their confidence, and nor will their midweek cup defeat to Brentford. In fact, City go into this game in the relegation zone, though it is early days in a long season and one win would see them shoot up the table

United's season hasn't been great either, and with both teams missing big players, we go somewhat into the unknown today, as two patched-up sides go for bragging rights in Manchester for the next few months at least.

2:00 pm. And here are the team sheets, fresh off the press. For the home side, similar injury problems to United have been experienced, so Andy Dibble is absent, and in comes elder statesman Paul Cooper, the 35-year-old expecting a busy afternoon. Clive Allen is out injured, while midfielder Neil McNab is ill and unable to play. And with their absentees, Brian McClair plays for United despite seven stitches in a head wound.

Manchester City team: Cooper, Fleming, Hinchcliffe, Bishop, Gayle, Redmond, White, Morley, Oldfield, Brightwell, Lane (Beckford, 79).

Manchester United team: Leighton, Anderson, Donaghy, Duxbury, Phelan, Pallister, Beardsmore, Ince, McClair, Hughes, Wallace.

Neil Midgley of Bolton is the referee.

2:10pm. United are yet to win away yet this season, after three attempts. In fact, City could actually go above their neighbours with a win today, though it would take victory by at least a four-goal margin to do that, so it's probably not worth spending too much time pondering that.

11	Manchester United	6	2	1	3	12	10	+2	7
12	Charlton Athletic	6	1	3	2	6	5	+1	6
13	Aston Villa	6	1	3	2	6	6	0	6
14	Queens Park Rangers	6	1	3	2	3	3	0	6
15	Nottingham Forest	6	1	3	2	7	8	-1	6
16	Wimbledon	6	1	3	2	4	6	-2	6
17	Crystal Palace	6	1	2	3	4	14	-10	5

| 18 | Manchester City | 6 | 1 | 1 | 4 | 5 | 9 | -4 | 4 |
| 19 | Tottenham Hotspur | 5 | 1 | 1 | 3 | 5 | 10 | -5 | 4 |

2:20 pm. United have been flashing the cash in the summer as they aim to become the top dogs in English football. They broke the British transfer record to complete the signing of Middlesbrough defender Gary Pallister in August, and he will feature today. It's been reported that Ferguson had set his sights on Fiorentina's Swedish centre-half Glenn Hysen, but after believing a deal to have been agreed, the player then stunned the United manager by choosing to sign for bitter rivals Liverpool instead. I'm not sure if that is true, but it makes for a good story.

Still United started the season in fine fettle with a 4-1 rout of league champions Arsenal at Old Trafford, with new buy Neil Webb scoring a lush volley to put the icing on the cake. That good start was not maintained however, with United going on to lose three of their next four league games, against the might of Crystal Palace, Derby, Everton and Norwich City. Not the stuff of potential champions.

To make matters worse, Ferguson lost Webb to an achilles tendon injury suffered on England duty after he had made just four appearances for United, then for good measure lost Bryan Robson and Steve Bruce to injury too. That opening day rout of Arsenal already seems a long time ago.
Still, they come into this game on the back of a 5-1 victory at home to Millwall in their previous league game.

2:35pm. The players have been out to warm up, but are back in their respective dressing rooms now. The ground is beginning to fill up, and the atmosphere is building nicely.

2:50 pm. Michael Knighton takes his seat, seemingly the new Manchester United chairman, and he seems to be enjoying his new status, happily signing autographs for those around him. I wonder what lies ahead for him? He'll want Alex Ferguson to up his game for starters.

2:55 pm. And the teams are out, and it seems everyone in the crowd is wearing their colours today in the pleasant Mancunian weather, the ground a swathe of blue and a little pocket of red. "We're the pride of Manchester," sing the home fans. We will see.

The usual hand-shakes and photographs take place, whilst Trevor Morley tries to keep Paul Lake calm by firing balls at his feet as hard as possible.

KICK OFF – MANCHESTER CITY V MANCHESTER UNITED
So here we go, as the 111th Manchester derby kicks off.

04:00: Little of note has happened yet, but United seem the more comfortable so far, and are enjoying time in City's half. For now though, both teams are playing within themselves, and are trying to settle into the match.

05:00: And the main talking point so far is off the field. There appears to be significant trouble in the North Stand, as rival fans throw punches, and as fans spill onto the field to avoid trouble. The referee has no option but to halt the game and call the players back to the dressing rooms. Just what we don't want to see on a day of great anticipation.

Plenty of police around the pitch now, trying to sort this out. The fighting was short-lived, but the pitch is not clear, and there are fans that need to be rehoused somewhere. I'm sure we'll be back underway soon though.

It is United fans who have bought tickets for the North stand that seem to have caused this fighting. They have been ushered elsewhere, and after nine minutes of stoppage in play, we seem ready to resume. Hopefully we'll just be talking about the football from now on.

07:00: The first chance of the game – almost. Hughes finds himself in acres of space on the left of the area, and his pass is heading for McClair until a vital interception by Gayle.

09:00: It's City's turn to waste an opportunity. Oldfield gets the ball out on the right and feeds White who surges into the area, but he puts a cross along the six yard line to no one in particular, when a cut back was the better option. Morley was well placed for that cut back, and you wonder if White was actually shooting. Badly.

11:00 GOAL – Manchester City 1 Manchester United 0. It's first blood to City. Hinchcliffe sprays a great ball out to White on the right wing. He cuts the ball back, and Pallister cannot reach it. It falls to Oldfield instead who slams the ball past Leighton. That has to go down as a mistake by Pallister, who really should have cut out the cross, but his positioning was poor.

12:00: GOAL – Manchester City 2 Manchester United 0. City fans go wild, and they probably can't believe their luck as shambolic defending from United again lets City double their lead. Donaghy dallied with the ball on the edge of his own area, was dispossessed by Morley who forced a good save from

Leighton. Lake picked up the ball, found space to force another save from Leighton, but Morley was the quickest to prod home the loose ball and City are in heaven. It's Morley's first goal since he clinched promotion at Bradford, and United have only themselves to blame.

25:00: United come oh so close to halving the deficit. A corner is not cleared by City, Cooper flaps at the ball and it falls for Viv Anderson, who prods towards goal, but Fleming manages to clear it off the line.

35:00: GOAL – Manchester City 3 Manchester United 0. And City are really in dreamland now! They have had to weather some intense pressure from United, but broke forward and Redmond fed Oldfield down the right channel. He escaped a sprawling Pallister, and chipped the ball into the area where Ian Bishop was steaming in to head the ball home. United are in utter disarray, and it's fast becoming an afternoon to forget for United's expensive acquisition Gary Pallister.

Half-time. **Manchester City 3 Manchester United 0**. I doubt even City's wildest optimists saw this coming, and City reach half-time with a comfortable three goal cushion. They have taken their chances, and taken advantage of some poor defending from their illustrious neighbours.

Analysis: United have been slow and sloppy at the back. City on the other hand have been rapier sharp onto the loose balls and must have surprised Alex Ferguson with a tenacity that has not been evident this season up to now. United started brightly, but the interruption in play seems to have really destroyed their concentration.
A real mountain for United to climb, although City are completely unaccustomed to leading their rivals like this, so an

early goal in the second half may yet bring a swift case of the jitters. United will be hoping this is the case. Meanwhile Ferguson will be looking at Gary Pallister, all £2.8 million of him, and hoping he can pull himself together in the second period.

The second half is underway. Can United get back into this?

48:00: Brightwell charges down the right and his cross seems to deflect off the arm of Mal Donaghy, but the referee waves away any penalty appeals as there seemed little intent. United have been porous on the road this season, conceding on average two goals a game, and they have now conceded three by the interval.

50:00: GOAL – Manchester City 3 Manchester United 1. Hope for Manchester United as a piece of class brings them back into the game. Hughes found space in midfield and fed Beardsmore on the right. He wriggled free and chipped the ball to the far post, where an acrobatic scissor kick from Hughes finds the back of the net. This game is not over yet.

Chance for United as Wallace dribbles into the penalty area form out on the left and lets fly, but Cooper is equal to it and saves well.

59:00: GOAL – Manchester City 4 Manchester United 1. United's comeback is short-lived, as City restore their three goal lead and surely ensure victory in the 11th Manchester derby. Lake burst into the area, forced a good save from Leighton, but the ball rebounded to Lake near the touchline. He calmly slotted it back to Oldfield to slot into a near-empty net. United players are claiming handball by Lake in the lead up to the goal, but the referee is not interested.

<u>Statistic</u>: It's the first time City have scored four goals in a league derby for 20 years.

Michael Knighton does not look too impressed sat in the crowd, as his expensively-assembled side fall to pieces before his eyes. He has been clutching his mobile phone throughout the match – he may have some important calls to make after full time.

62:00: GOAL – Manchester City 5 Manchester United 1. And what a way to hammer home a derby day advantage, as City pile on the humiliation with a wonderful 5th goal. Bishop sprays the ball out wide to David White, he crosses instantly and Hinchcliffe charges into the far post area to bullet a header home. A dream day for Manchester City.

And that's a true collector's item on a day when virtually everything is going right for City – a header from Andy Hinchcliffe. There can't have been many of them in the history books, if any.

64:00: The only question remaining now is how many more goals do City have in them? Excuse the terrible pun, but it has turned into a Maine Road Massacre – you can have that for free.

68:00: Some United fans have already left, but unless my ears deceive me, a few that have remained are chanting "Fergie Out!". No doubt he's under pressure after this performance, against a team that cost less than one of his defenders, and a few match programmes have been thrown onto the pitch from a disgruntled away end.

69:00: Almost a consolation for United. McClair battles well down the right and feeds Hughes, who returns it to the Scot, but his pass trickles across the six yard line and past the advancing United players.

71:00: Manchester United substitution: Sharp is on for Beardsmore – not that it can make much difference.

80:00: Manchester City substitution: Beckford is on for Lake – not surprisingly City's energetic midfielder gets a superb send-off from the home crowd, though he probably won't notice. He is forced off after a poor, crude challenge from Mike Phelan which has injured him enough to force him off, and left a few stud marks for good measure. Phelan not taking defeat too well it seems.
Physio Roy Bailey leads Lake tentatively off the pitch and back towards the Main Stand. And then off down the tunnel, no doubt to place a much-needed ice pack on his leg.

81:00: Got the attendance here – a packed Maine Road as you'd expect, and a crowd of 43,246. Segregation alone has prevented the crowd being higher, not that it seems to have been of much use today.

83:00: United spring forward with the dangerous Wallace, but Cooper is alert to the danger and just gets to the ball before McClair.

87:00: Not surprisingly, the match is petering out now, the United players well aware that the game is now a lost cause, and their faces will be as red as their shirts. For City, it is a job magnificently done.

FULL TIME – Manchester City 5 Manchester United 1.
That's it, and City have recorded their biggest ever derby win here at Maine Road. Their poor start to the season can be

forgotten for now, after an incredible victory that few would have predicted.

And amazingly because City have won by a four-goal margin, they go above United in the table.

The City players show their thanks to the capacity crowd, whilst naturally the United players can't wait to get back to the dressing room. "We love you City, we do," sing the crowd as the players troop off and the fans get their breath back.

Well that was rather unexpected, but we have been treated to another Manchester derby full of excitement and incident.

For City, this was the boost their season needed, after their worst start to a season in nine years. It's now up to them to take this form forward and climb further up the table, and away from the relegation zone. For United, the worst possible day, and the season stumbles along as before. Talk of a title challenge from their expensively assembled squad seems a million miles away right now, and their manager will come under renewed pressure, especially with an ambitious new owner waiting in the wings.

And here's a random thought – did the injury problems for City actually benefit them in the end? Due to absences, there were six boyhood blues in City's squad today, and the home team were clearly more up for it than their opponents. Apparently Tony Book was in the home dressing room too pre-match, firing up the troops. He should charge good money for his speeches if today is anything to go by.

Anyway, manager Mel Machin has been supplying a few words of wisdom outside the ground: "It's obviously a big lift for the boys, because there's a lot of pressure because of what has been spent across the road, but it doesn't buy you success as everybody knows. I felt today the writing was on the wall for us to get a good result, probably our best time to play them. Before today's game we were playing very well, but the results weren't coming for us...I might have a couple of drinks tonight."

As for the away manager - "If you give away silly goals you haven't got a chance. It was like climbing a glass mountain," said Alex Ferguson. Well indeed.

And that's the end of a fascinating day in Manchester, as the boys in blue thrashed the red devils to heap more pressure on their ambitious manager and prospective new owner. Expect a response from United in the coming weeks, and for the blue half of Manchester, it's important to kick on, as this was only three points after all. Still, for City fans that's something to think about on another day, and they will have a good night and smug faces in the office tomorrow.

Manchester City 2 Liverpool 2
Sunday 5th May 1996.

"And Niall Quinn sprints from the tunnel to frantically tell the City players they need another goal!"

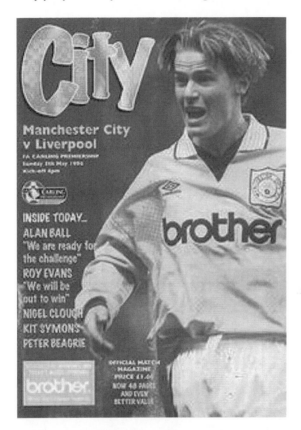

2:30 pm. A good Sunday afternoon from Maine Road, as the 1995/6 Premier League season draws to a close with much at stake at the lower end of the table. This is where the interest lies on the final day, and especially so here at Maine Road, as Manchester City find themselves in a three-way scrap to avoid relegation.

City have given themselves a chance of staying up by winning their last 2 games 1-0, at home to Sheffield Wednesday and away to Aston Villa. Their performance at Villa Park should give them the confidence to get the result today, against a Liverpool side with little to play for.

And Liverpool's attitude could be crucial. Whatever the result, they will finish 3rd, so you could argue they won't be trying too hard. Newcastle cannot be caught in 2nd place in the table, nor can Aston Villa in 4th position catch Liverpool.

For the home team, if it doesn't go City's way today, they'll probably be glad to see the back of Liverpool. They lost 4-0 at Anfield in the League Cup 3rd round, which almost seems like a good result compared to the 6-0 tonking they received in the league back in October – and those two results were just three days apart. A chance perhaps to put things right today, but have they left it too late?

So where did it all go wrong for City? When Alan Ball took over last summer, he said his job was "the envy of millions". I would suggest that envy has somewhat waned over subsequent months. Now it's more a poisoned chalice, but Ball has one more chance of redemption.
Part of the problem has been the sense of transition at the club. Some elder statesmen have moved on, younger players have replaced them, and there is a lack of stability and cohesion on and off the pitch.
Looking at City's season, it would be easy to blame their predicament on their atrocious start to the season, and that would be fair enough. Without a win in their opening eleven games, the team have been under immense pressure from the start, especially as there was much criticism directed towards

Chairman Francis Lee for appointing a friend to the manager's role.

However, after that appalling start, City rallied soon after, winning four of their next five games, which saw them climb out of the relegation zone – so you could argue it was the inability to maintain that form, or anything close to it, which has seen them fighting for their lives. A terrible December, a pretty average January, and rather poor form until a fortnight ago leads us to today, and a desperate need for victory. Throw in a cup exit to Manchester United, helped by the dodgiest of all dodgy penalty calls, and I would say with some confidence that this season could have gone better for City, all things considered.

That Manager of the Month award for November for Alan Ball seems a long time ago right now.

2:45 pm. It seems a long way away for Francis Lee too. Lee took over in February 1994 and two weeks later he said: "This will be the happiest club in the land. The players will be the best paid and we'll drink plenty of champagne, celebrate and sing until we're hoarse."

Well it hasn't quite gone to plan. Lee might have made progress on improving the ground, but the team have not followed suit. Relegation will be disastrous for Lee's plans to make City a force again. The fans have showed great faith in Lee delivering, but it seems that whilst the players, managers and owners may change, some things stay the same at City, most notably underachievment.

2:50 pm. For Liverpool too, perhaps there is a sense of disappointment as the season draws to an end. For many, they were the team to beat when the season began, bolstered by record signing Stan Collymore, so whilst they will finish in their highest position for five seasons, there will surely be thoughts about what could have been. A poor November did for them, but the truth is they were out of the race for all of this year. What's more, it will be their fierce rivals "down the East Lancs" who will take the title, and their season will rest on how they do against United in the upcoming FA Cup Final. Still, European football is guaranteed for next season, so there's a positive.

But today they must be seen to be putting in the effort, as to not do so would be unfair on City's relegation rivals – and I think we will see as much commitment as ever from the visitors – manager Roy Evans should see to that. In fact, he is quoted on the front of today's match programme saying that they will be out to win this match – but then he's hardly going to say anything different is he?

Still, manager Alan Ball is in bullish mood, as you would expect. "I am confident we will stay up, because we have prepared well and we are ready."

3:00 pm. So with an hour to go, the all-important teams are announced.

City team:
Immel, Summerbee, Brown, Curle, Symons, I Brightwell, Clough, Quinn, Rosler, Lomas, Kinkladze.

Liverpool team:
James, Jones, Ruddock, Babb, Wright, Redknapp, 16 Thomas, McAteer, McManaman, Fowler, Rush.

Three substitutes each for both sides of course, and will they have a say on how this game goes? For City, the subs are Phillips, Kavelashvili and Frontzeck.

Liverpool's three subs are Kennedy, Warner and Matteo.

A poignant day for Ian Rush, who will play for Liverpool for the final time and is fittingly made captain for the occasion.

And that is not a bad team for City, one that makes you wonder how they have got to this point.

3:10 pm. City will be glad to be playing at home – the bad news for them is that Coventry City and Southampton are too, against Leeds and Wimbledon respectively. Both teams are just safe from relegation, so all three teams fighting for their lives today will be playing rather disinterested opposition.

3:30 pm. So whilst there are a number of teams who could theoretically be relegated by the end of the afternoon, it is Manchester City that are in the weakest position. With one relegation spot up for grabs, Sheffield Wednesday are probably safe, being two points ahead of Manchester City, Coventry City and Southampton. A point for Wednesday will ensure survival for them due to their superior goal difference.

More realistic is to presume that one of the remaining teams fills that final spot, and it is Manchester City that currently fill it as they have the worst goal difference. So their task today is simple –better the result of either Coventry City or Southampton (or both). Fail to do that and they are down. Theoretically a win could see City still go down, but I would think it's fairly probable that three points will probably keep

City up, so they really have to go out there today looking for a win, then hope for the best.

3:55 pm. Even before the game begins, there is sadness in the air. The players of both teams stand silently around the centre circle, as an impeccable minute's silence is held for the late Peter Swales, who died only three days ago. There is a certain irony that the man who was convinced he would leave the club with City bigger than their neighbours United, did not survive to see his team possibly be relegated to the 2nd tier of English football. You might have worried that the silence would not be observed, but for all the controversy of Swales' reign, and the protests he drew from many City fans, the time for rancour is long gone, and I think that many fans realise that whilst it didn't often go to plan, Swales was a true blue and had the good of the club at heart along with everyone else – what a shame that his time at the club ended in such ugly scenes, and he was a broken a man for the rest of his life. What's more, Francis Lee's reign has shown that the grass is not always greener on the other side of the fence, and you should be careful what you wish for. How City fans must pine for 4th and 5th place finishes now.

Naturally the City players are wearing black armbands today.

With the silence brought to a close by the whistle of the referee, we are ready to get underway. A big crowd is in boisterous form, and are getting behind the team, keen to see their team start next season in the top flight.

KICK OFF – MANCHESTER CITY V LIVERPOOL

04:00: The first chance goes to Liverpool. City look nervous, as shown by another misplaced pass, this time by Nigel Clough, who passes straight to Steve McManaman. He surges forward, and his pass just outside the area falls for Ian Rush, who as he lines up for goal has the ball nipped off his feet and it goes behind for a corner.

06:00: GOAL – Manchester City 0 Liverpool 1. Just what City did not need, as they fall behind as only they can. From the resultant corner, Steve McManaman gets the ball on the left of the area, jinks past his man and fires in a low cross, but Steve Lomas, the hero of last week, can only divert the ball into his own net. A disastrous start from City, who are doing a great job of shooting themselves in the foot here. Still, plenty of time to go.

12:00: And that is so close to an equalizer for City. Summerbee finds room down the right and puts in a good cross to the far post. Not surprisingly Niall Quinn rises highest but can only head against the bar. He is quickest to the rebound but his second header is saved by James and cleared. That probably should have been a goal.

18:00: And yet again, somehow Niall Quinn has failed to draw City level. A high cross is completely missed by Mark Wright, but the ball bounces off a well-placed Quinn back to the Liverpool defender. He however contrives to immediately give the ball away, and the ball is threaded through to Quinn in front of goal, but his shot flicks the body of the diving James and goes millimetres over the bar.

Having watched the replay, I'm not sure how the ball managed to go over the bar, but it did, and City still search for that elusive equalizer.

22:00: This really isn't looking like it will be City's day. Quinn lobs a beautiful chipped cross to the far post, James comes out, misses the ball and takes out a Liverpool defender, and at the far post, Uwe Rosler somehow manages to head wide with the goal at his mercy. Huge, huge miss.

30:00: And from player incompetence to referee incompetence. Kinkladze chips a nice pass to Summerbee who is clearly taken down by Neil Ruddock inside the penalty area. The referee agrees it is a foul – yet amazingly gives a free kick on the edge of the area. He must be the only person in the stadium who couldn't see where that foul occurred. Ruddock was stood outside the area, but Summerbee was entirely inside it when Ruddock's leg extended and tripped him up. Not the sort of decision City need right now.

Even Ruddock knew that was a penalty, and he looks as surprised as the rest of us as the referee indicates a free-kick.

31:00: The resultant free kick from Kinkladze strikes the wall. City will rightly feel cheated there, and the referee Steven Lodge was perfectly placed to see what happened. Still, Liverpool are clearly here for the taking, so City need to keep their heads up here.

41:00: GOAL – Manchester City 0 Liverpool 2. And that sums up how the day is going for City as relegation creeps ever closer. Liverpool break, and Steve McManaman feeds Ian Rush 40 yards out. He advances and from outside the area unleashes a shot, which takes a big deflection off the foot of Keith Curle and flies into the back of the net. Disaster for City, and Liverpool are two up without really trying.

That's Rush's 7th of the season, and his 346th in Liverpool colours.

Nothing more to report in that first half, which can only mean one thing...

Half-time. Manchester City 0 Liverpool 2.

The referee blows his whistle and that half could not have gone much worse for the hosts. For much of the game they were the dominant side, but they have repeatedly failed to take their chances, have been let down by the referee and also shot themselves in the foot, both Liverpool goals coming off the feet of City players.

The only hope that remains for City is that their relegation rivals are not winning either, otherwise the fight would be pretty much over. Unfortunately for City they aren't losing either, both games still goalless, so as it stands City would need to win here today and thus score three goals in the second half. Anything's possible, and things can change quickly on the last day of a relegation scrap, but it looks pretty bleak for the Citizens at the moment.

And as the teams come out for the second half, there is a change afoot for the visitors.

Substitution for Liverpool – Kennedy is on for Redknapp.

SECOND HALF

So, the 2nd half is underway, and Manchester City need a near-miracle now. Everything has gone wrong for them, but they need to keep trying, as Liverpool certainly allowed them chances in the first half.

50:00: Rosler has the first sight of goal of the half, and lets fly from outside the area, but James saves comfortably, though Kennedy has to complete a clearance.

55:00: Another chance goes begging. Quinn feeds Kinkladze who wriggles into the area on the left, but with the whites of David James' eyes in his sight, he blazes over. City are running out of lives.

59:00: Substitution. On comes Martin "Buster" Phillips (for Niall Quinn0, who Alan Ball once rather optimistically predicted would be the country's first £10m player. I'd say that looks unlikely now. City fans would settle for him making a difference today and dragging City back into this game. That would be worth a few million in itself.

The attendance has been announced as 31,436, which is a full house as we expected, and thus is the biggest crowd of the season at Maine Road.

63:00: It's already been mentioned by me, but is worth repeating. You get a very strong feeling that many of the Liverpool players would be happy for City to stay up, and will be as bemused as most of us at how they are two goals ahead considering how accommodating they have been. City have really missed an opportunity here.

68:00: Substitution: Kavelashvili on for Clough. An extra striker on for City, which makes sense as the situation gets desperate, but a bit of an unknown quantity to be honest - but maybe that is what City need.

70:00: PENALTY MANCHESTER CITY – a glimmer of hope for the home side. It takes a bit of magic from Kinkladze to finally bring that hope, a solo run into the area brought to an end after the referee adjudges Neil Ruddock to have blocked him off. Ruddock gets a yellow card for his efforts.

No surprise that Ruddock was the transgressor there. He has resembled a lumbering pub player for much of the day, and that really should be the 2nd penalty he has conceded today.

71:00: GOAL – Manchester City 1 Liverpool 2. Uwe Rosler fires the ball down the middle true and hard for his 13th goal of the season, and City are back in it. A frantic 20 minutes awaits us here. As it stands City still need another two goals, so it remains an uphill task.

73:00: City pushing forward as much as possible now, with plenty of urgency in their play. They'd do well not to look at the clock though, as time ebbs away. Summerbee is looking lively down the right though, and he wins a corner.

78:00: GOAL – Manchester City 2 Liverpool 2. Well, well, well! Now we have a finale in prospect! A City corner reaches Phillips on the left, and his cross evades two Liverpool defenders and James, and in sneaks Kit Symons at the far post to ram the ball home from close range. Hope for City.

"It's not the despair, Laura. I can take the despair. It's the hope I can't stand." Brian Stimpson (John Cleese), Clockwise.
Well I don't remember who Laura was, but the sentiment stands. The City players have given their fans hope, but will it be all in vain? We're about to find out.

84:00: Either I have slipped into a weird dream, or Manchester City have access to time-travel or better communications than me. Steve Lomas appears to be holding the ball near the corner as a disinterested Liverpool player considers whether to tackle him, which can only mean one thing – the City team (or Lomas at least) have been informed that one of their relegation rivals is losing, and think that a draw is enough.

84:30: Well that's news to us. As far as we are aware, both the Coventry and Southampton games remain goalless, meaning City have to win. Where are they getting their information from? More to the point, what on earth are they doing? This is utterly ridiculous.

85:00: Nope, there have DEFINITELY been no goals elsewhere, so whoever informed the City players otherwise either has rather a warped sense of humour or is an undercover United/Coventry/Southampton fan. The ball is no longer in the corner, but City's urgency remains at a worryingly low level. Attack!!!!

86:00: **Astonishing scenes here**. Niall Quinn has appeared from up the tunnel (looking very dapper in beige slacks and matching shirt I should add) and is waving furiously at the City players. He seems to be the only City player who knows that as it stands, City need another goal or they are down.

87:00: Well the good news is that the City players seems to have got the message now – namely that they need another goal. The bad news is that their time-wasting has knocked another few minutes off the clock, and that's the last thing they need with time quickly running out. We're approaching last-chance saloon territory here, unless there is late drama elsewhere. A goal at any of the three games could change everything.

So to recap: needing a goal to stay up, against opposition showing little interest in competing for the ball, City decided to shield the ball near the corner flag. You really couldn't make it up.

88:00: One final chance for City? Whether it is or not, it is not taken. City get a free kick on the left, Kinkladze puts it into the area, and Summerbee rises at the far post and heads it back across goal. Unfortunately for City, it is inches behind Kavelashveli, and he cannot get his foot round it, and the ball is cleared.

90:00: It's desperate now, but City cannot string together a good period of play and are looking too panicked to change that.

Full Time: Manchester City 2 Liverpool 2 – as it stands, Manchester City are relegated.

That is it. The sound of the referee's whistle is a dagger through the heart of everyone at City, and you can feel the despondency around the ground. City appear to have fallen short.

And confirmation that **City are relegated** – Coventry and Southampton have both drawn, so City are down on goal difference. A disastrous and sad day for all those involved with City, and the lack of urgency towards the end, though in truth it probably wouldn't have made any difference, certainly did not help matters.

6:00pm. We're hearing that Niall Quinn, the only person who seemed to know the score(s), got his information from a police monitor in the tunnel. Perhaps City could use them more prominently in the future, it might make all the difference next time.

6:10pm. The players are shattered and dejected in the tunnel, probably wondering if an end of season lap of honour is really a good idea. Nothing really went their way today, though they didn't help themselves at times.

6:20 pm. Alan Ball: "There's not a lot you can say (to the players). They've had a go today, but it's over the season, and unfortunately our shocking start we've paid dearly for in the end."

6:30pm. Niall Quinn: "There's a huge cloud over the club. The players can only apologise...perhaps for how we started the year. At the end of the day, the buck stops with us. Recent form counts for nothing now, nobody ever told me there'd be days like this, and it's hard to swallow."

6:40 pm. This will hit plenty of the players hard, none more so than Steve Lomas, who has been at the centre of everything on the pitch in the last week ago. But for a player who has been at the club since the age of twelve, this will be tough for him to take.

A bit more from City's beleaguered manager.
"We will come back strong. It's going to be a long hard season, but sometimes it's for the best. I'm sure we can bounce back."

Shades of the "I enjoyed the match" quote after the pummelling at Anfield? Either way, I'm not sure relegation is "for the best".

"I'm proud of them (the players). It just wasn't to be. You could not have written a script that saw us give away two goals and have a penalty disallowed. But it's not just down to today. It's over a year and we paid dearly for our start when we only took two points from 12 games."

Outside the ground, there is naturally a sombre mood. Just seen a careworn City fan approach another adult with his young son and ask: "How's the youngster taking it?"
Father: "He's very young. He doesn't really understand what's happened."
Careworn fan: "Oh he will in time. He will."

They say days like this make you tougher. Small comfort I imagine. They'll be back though, one day.

And then there's the United fan on BBC Five Live's phone-in with a semi-gloat at his neighbours' demise: "I'm really sad they've gone down. Well, it's six points isn't it?"

So, tough times ahead for City. Francis Lee will have to decide whether Alan Ball is the right man to lead City back to the big time, and there may be a need to ship out many of the big earners. For now the key is to ensure promotion at the first attempt, as City fans look forward to games against the likes of Grimsby Town and Port Vale rather than Liverpool or United. In a season when their illustrious neighbours excelled once more, the pain will be felt even deeper for all City fans tonight.

Will they ever get it right and challenge United? Not in the foreseeable future.

Sunday 30th May 1999
Division Two Play-Off Final. Manchester City v Gillingham

"Well, it's not over until the final whistle. And City here looking for an opening. It's Dickov again!!! Can you believe it?!"

Welcome to a damp and grey Wembley Stadium. It is (almost literally) do or die for Manchester City this afternoon, while for Gillingham the pressure is more or less off. City's season "down among the dead men" of Division Three, as we used to call it in simpler unreconstructed times has been, at times, an absolutely excruciating thing to watch. At other times, it has been merely very painful indeed.

The stakes are what you might want to call "high". For City they really couldn't be any higher. Relegated to the third tier for the first time in their long and illustrious history a year ago at Stoke's Britannia Stadium, Joe Royle's side stand ninety minutes from immediate promotion back to the *Land of the Half Alive,* occupied by the likes of Stockport, Bury, Port Vale and Crewe. Yes, that's right, Manchester City, league champions, cup winners, European victors, home to Colin Bell and Francis Lee, are this afternoon tussling for the right to jump "up" to the level of Bury and Stockport County.

Conversely, they also stand ninety minutes from having it confirmed that they will stay a second consecutive year down in the basement with York City, Wrexham and Macclesfield Town and one wonders whether the club will survive all that that little lot means. The players too may not want to contemplate another season playing at Sincil Bank.

For City followers that have wandered through the barren times with the club in 98-99, this must feel truly awful. Nothing to celebrate about, this, just an attempt to claw back some pride and get back into the top two divisions as quickly as possible.

With the club leeching cash, they have been saved by the fans' loyalty this season. Averaging an incredible 28,000 at home throughout the season, they have filled stadia from Walsall to Bournemouth and from Lincoln to Wycombe. The 32,471 that packed Maine Road for the final home game of the season proper against York City (4-0) was the club's highest home crowd for five years. There were another 31, 305 there to see them squeeze past Wigan Athletic in a breathtaking play-off semi-final second leg. Don't forget this long and winding story began back in August at a sun-drenched Maine Road when Blackpool were put to the sword 3-0 in front of 32,134. It has been a season of frayed nerves for the faithful but my word they have turned up in serious numbers this season to partake in a carnival of masochistic pleasure.

There will be nearly 40,000 City fans at Wembley today and only the Football League's amazing decision to grant opponents Gillingham 34,000 tickets (home average this season at the Priestfield Stadium is a paltry 6,748), has stopped City from filling the place by themselves.

It had been argued strongly by the Manchester Evening News and their City correspondent Richard Burgess that City should get 59,000 and Gillingham 13,000, based on these crowd figures. Whilst that was never going to happen, City did request 45,000 and were turned down after Gillingham chairman Paul Scally said they would be able to sell all 35,000 tickets offered to them. That is going to make for a lot of City fans watching on tv and a lot of Gillingham fans who have never seen "their" team play before. Expect to see a number of Gillingham fans in newly pressed replica shirts this afternoon, then, and one or two who might not know the players' names beyond the prolific scoring duo of Carl Asaba and Andy Hessethaler.

Let's just look at the two sides facing each other today in the classic haves and have-nots mode that the papers so love:

Honours : CITY: Div One champions twice, FA Cup 4 times, European Cup Winners Cup once, League Cup twice, Division Two champs six times. **GILLINGHAM**: Div Four champs 1964

Ground capacity: Maine Road 32,000   Priestfield 10,000

Record attendance: City 85,000 Gillingham 23,000

Record transfer fee received: City – Georgi Kinkladze £4.9 Gillingham £1.2 Ade Akinbiyi

Manager: City, ex-England and Everton striker Joe Royle

Gillingham: Harry Redknapp's old Bournemouth assistant manager Tony Pulis

Here is what protagonists in the two camps have to say about today's big occasion:

City manager Joe Royle: *"City have not been one of the top six clubs for a long time, but this is still one of the big six clubs. The infrastructure of the place is geared towards Europe rather than the second division. Aston Villa had to take some of this medicine. We've got to look at that and think it's a possibility. This club has been majoring in disappointment and underachievement for a long time but sooner or later someone's* going to get it right here and I hope that it's me. With the right rules laid down we'll be on our way".

Gillingham chairman Paul Scally: *"We talk the same language (he and Tony Pulis). We're both a bit anti-establishment. I think we could have sold 100,000 tickets for this one".*

City winger Terry Cooke: *"I want to give the blue half of Manchester something to cheer about as well. Whatever has been going on across town with United, City fans just want it all to work out for them after so many heartaches".*

Ex-City Chairman Francis Lee: *"I used to chew my finger nails down to the bone. It was a seven day a week job and there were a thousand things to deal with. I put a lot into it but eventually I just thought "to hell with this". I enjoy life too much to put up with this. I never want to be chairman ever again".*

Ex-Manchester Evening News City correspondent Peter Gardner, writing in The People in August: *"City should be the class act of the Second. Whether they are hinges on an ability to come to terms with football at a level where thud and blunder is as much part of the game as the class and skill a club of City's reputation should still genuinely possess".*

Well, much like Franny Lee, there are 40,000 people with a Mancunian accent wandering around with very short finger nails here this afternoon. I saw one little boy and he couldn't even break into his crisp packet, poor chump. His dad couldn't help either, but that wasn't because of a finger nail issue, more to do with a lack of balance and ability to focus with at least one eye. It is that sort of an occasion here today.

City only travelled down yesterday. As Joe Royle said *"We're not going to a hotel in Berkshire. We want everything to be normal"*. Not sure how possible "normal" is at City right now, but Royle and his side will be hoping for a normal enough 90 minutes here without too much high blood pressure. If that is the case, then it will mean his City side have sailed back into the second tier and can prepare a budget to get them even higher. If not, there will be a drip feed needed for those 40,000 fans tonight. By the way that figure of 28,000 home average attendance is the highest at Maine Road since 1982. Incredible.

1400 We are speculating because the team sheets have not yet reached us, but these are the two sides we expect to see this afternoon: City expect to have Andy Morrison back in defence, probably in place of Tony Vaughan. Gillingham are also likely to be at full strength with that prolific strike partnership of Bob Taylor and Carl Asaba, which has torn defences to threads this season.

The clubs have of course already met twice this season and this is what happened:

Saturday 21st November 1998, Maine Road
Manchester City 0 Gillingham 0
Saturday 17th April 1999, Priestfield Stadium
Gillingham 0 Manchester City 2 (Cooke, Horlock)

Final Division Two League Table looked like this at the end of battle:

1 Fulham	46	31	8	7	79-32	101
2 Walsall	46	26	9	11	63-47	87
3 Man City	46	22	16	8	69-33	82
4 Gillingham	46	22	14	10	75-44	80

5 Preston	46	22	13	11	78-50	79
6 Wigan	46	22	10	14	75-48	76

1430 Teams are now in and there are no surprises. City line up like this:

Weaver: Crooks, Edghill, Wiekens, Morrison; Horlock, Brown, Whitley; Dickov, Goater, Cooke

Weaver is 20, Crooks 21 and Edghill 24, although he and Michael Brown are the only survivors from City's Premier League days in the mid 90s, so there might be some nerves in there. City have two links to neighbours United, who set the bar high this week by completing the treble in Barcelona with that last gasp Champions League win over Bayern Munich: Shaun Goater was an apprentice there before heading off to Rotherham to learn his goal-scoring trade and Terry Cooke moved between the clubs as recently as last January in a loan deal after spending time out at Wrexham recovering from knee ligament damage.

And Gillingham look like this:
Bartram; Ashby, Pennock, Butters, Patterson; Smith, Hessenthaler, Galloway, Southall; Asaba, Taylor.

Goalkeeper Vince Bartram is a close friend of City's Paul Dickov, who was in fact Best Man at the Gillingham man's wedding. They know each other from being at Arsenal's academy in the early nineties. Who will be raising a toast to the other tonight, I wonder?

1440 Last stragglers heading up a wet and gloomy Wembley Way now. Most fans are inside and making a fair bit of noise. You have to wonder for those City fans how many are experiencing Wembley for the first time. You can bet they did not envisage this as being their opportunity to break that particular duck. For every single Gillingham fan, it is their first time here. It's easy to see how City might lose a generation of young local fans to treble winners United, but it's heartening to see so many kids here today wearing the sky blue favours. Perhaps they dream of the unreachable, parity with United, but there are some more downbeat objectives to achieve here first.

1450 Wembley now packed to the rafters and, as the teams come out they look tiny, enveloped by smoke and tinsel. Fatboy Slim booms out from the Wembley speakers and the old ground shudders to yet another day of reckoning. Only for City this is very much more important than that. Incredible noise swelling up from both ends. City fans in a visible, if not overwhelming, majority here. A sea of flags fluttering in the thick smoke that has been produced by lines of fireworks going off. Wasn't like this when Billy Bremner and Bobby Kerr walked out into the light in 1973 I can tell you. Bob Stokoe's gabardine mac and trilby combo has also been eschewed by today's managers, with both men in smart suits and ties.

Ready for the off, great atmosphere, rain tumbling down, Fatboy Slim quiet at last.

1455 Joe Royle and Tony Pulis lead the sides to the usual positions in front of the royal box, which today is spectacularly bereft of top rank royals. The House of Windsor not so very interested in a third tier play off, as you might imagine. Give them the chance to shake David Beckham's hand and they're here in their droves, but eye to eye with Andy Morrison, it's Earl Grey and buttered crumpets at the Palace. Instead Joe Royle has to suffice with the marketing manager of Nationwide to introduce to his troops. Andy Morrison looks suitably unimpressed with this. Did he just mouth to Royle, "where's the Duke of Edinburgh?". Don't disappoint Andy Morrison, whatever you do.

Joe Royle's mind might well be going back to the last time City won at Wembley. He would remember it well, because he was playing! 1976 League Cup final against Newcastle, won by that incredible overhead kick by Dennis Tueart, who is also here today in his capacity of venerable elder statesman and taking his seat up in the stands with the other City directors. Two more of that side, Willie Donachie and Asa Hartford, make up part of City's backroom staff today.

Some serious faces in the two line-ups. That old maxim of watching the two teams walk out at Wembley and the one whose players are busy waving to the crowd is the one who will lose doesn't really hold much weight today. Very few waves, lot of frowns and wet fringes. Paul Dickov resembling a poodle coming out of the bath already.

The Wembley pitch looks good but there was the third division play off yesterday, played in bright sunshine incidentally, but it was followed by a tropical storm in this part of north London and it has really thrown it down here this morning too, so we can expect what the experts might call a "slick surface" this afternoon. If there are any ball skills to be revealed, they might quickly be snuffed out by "the difficult surface, Terry".

It's either a trick of the light or Tony Pulis has miraculously changed from a man in a suit and tie to one wearing tracksuit bottom, a sweatshirt and a natty pair of oversized round glasses. How or where he did that, I am not quite sure.

00:24 PENALTY CLAIM IN FIRST MINUTE! And it's a good one. Dickov wriggles through into the box, creating panic among the Gillingham defenders and, as he turns and loops the ball over his own shoulder, Ashby appears to knock it away with his arm. *He does knock it away with his arm!!* Referee Mark Halsey is unimpressed but that looks like a penalty from here. What a let-off for the Kent side. 30 seconds on the clock! Drama has arrived, wandered in and taken a front row seat already.

02:00 YELLOW CARD PENNOCK. Crazy start to this game with the ball pinging around like a silver bullet. Adrian Pennock upends Dickov, who is everywhere in the opening exchanges and goes straight into Mr Halsey's engagement diary. Fair to say the game has not calmed down yet, but then we are barely two minutes in. As expected the surface is greasy and the players are sliding around a little too.

03:00 First proper chance and it's at the other end, where the busy, hunched figure of Hessenthaler squares a free kick to the centrally located Guy Butters. The defender takes an agricultural swipe at the ball and swots it wide of the falling Nicky Weaver's right hand post.

04:15 Now Weaver gets a proper feel of the ball himself, as Smith's tame shot goes along the ground and is gathered by the City keeper. Good, strong start by Gillingham, this. Early impressions are that Dickov intends to be a total pest to the Gillingham defence today and that Bob Taylor may have met his match in Andy Morrison at the other end. The City man is built like a brick outhouse and, although he is feeling a bruised hamstring, he'll be a tough barrier to get around for Taylor and Asaba today.

07:00 Another dangerous break for Gillingham, this time down the left, as Southall makes progress towards the edge of the box. As he arrives in the danger area, Lee Crooks slips over at just the wrong moment and he's through. Ball is cleared hastily into touch just before Taylor and Asaba can lay claim to it.

08:00 Jeff Whitely wallops his shot high over the bar for City. That's a bit of a Whitley speciality, it must be said.

10:35 REALLY CLOSE CALL: Gillingham closer than ever as Galloway brings down a deep cross from the right and hits a left footer which is curling inside Weaver's post, but draws a flying save from the young City keeper. Brighter start goes to Gillingham. City hoofing it long, but to Dickov instead of Goater. Butters and Pennock will eat those high balls up all afternoon, if they are aimed at Dickov, who comes up to their waistbands and no further.

17:00 NOW CITY GO CLOSE!! Best chance for Royle's men so far, as Lee Crooks advances from right back, picking up a loose ball after good build up play from Paul Dickov and Shaun Goater and hits a daisy-cutter just wide of Bartram's right hand post. Only one City goal so far for Crooks and it was a similarly low angled effort at Saltergate, Chesterfield at the beginning of March. This one just misses though.

24:00 EVEN CLOSER CITY! Edghill trying to batter his way through at the front of the eighteen yard box, centrally positioned. The ball squirms free to Dickov on the left, who produce a delicate high chip – is it a cross, is it a shot, is it a wedding present? – which floats past Bartram and misses the outstretched boot of Kevin Horlock by not more than two inches.

27:00 HORLOCK FOILED AGAIN Closer still they get and it's that man Kevin Horlock again, this time with a firm, diving header, blocked at point blank range by Vince Bartram. Clever cross in from the right by Terry Cooke, after he had been put clear into space down the right channel by the tireless Paul Dickov. Space is certainly at a premium here and that was as good a chance as we've seen so far. Unfortunately for City the chances are falling to the wrong people. Shaun Goater hasn't had a sniff of an opportunity yet and he can score with any part of his body.

35:00 TEMPERS FRAYING And it's Paul Dickov again at the centre of affairs, as you would expect from the fiery little Scot. Not for the first time this afternoon, Dickov is complaining to Mr Halsey about flying elbows, this time it's about a particularly sharp one belonging to Barry Ashby. Ashby retaliates to Dickov's choice words and the Scot then moves on to a close clinch with Nicky Southall. Mr Halsey is there with a soothing word or two and it all ends with a very civil handshake.

38:10 GOAL GILLINGHAM!!! But hold onto your hats, it's offside. And clearly so. Hessenthaler gets the ball across deep to Taylor but the big striker's somewhat non-balletic attempt at a volley cannons forward to Asaba, who is not expecting such an unusual goal attempt and is clearly offside. It was the shot from Taylor that went wrong and there was no hint that he was trying to pass to his forward partner, but nevertheless, no goal. The ball moves straight up to the other end and Edghill, of all people, has a close range header into the side netting. Things hotting up as the half draws to a conclusion, but still all the wrong people getting the chances for City: Edghill, Horlock and Crooks could start a Goalscorers' Aacdemy and few would turn up for advice.

45:00+2 HALF TIME - MANCHESTER CITY 0-0 GILLINGHAM.
Half time analysis: Combative, fast-moving first half between
two evenly matched sides that were separated by 82 league
places as recently as six years ago. City finished 9th in the
Premier League the season Gillingham were next to bottom of
Division Four. That represents an alarming change of fortune for
both clubs, doesn't it?

Brighter start by Gillingham, but the better chances have fallen
to City. Dickov fully involved but Shaun Goater is not and that
might be the difference so far between City actually capitalising
on some of these opportunities or not. Whitely twice firing
over, Horlock twice close and Crooks and Edgill just wide, but
none of these are recognised goalscorers, as I said. Joe Royle
must find a way of getting his big striker more involved in the
second period. Southall and Butters have done an excellent job
in shackling the dangerman Goater, it has to be said. No space
whatsoever for the big Bermudian so far.

46:00 Second Half: Pouring with rain again as the second half
gets under way with Smith and Hessenthaler, who sound like
gun manufacturers in the Wild West. If there's a shoot-out, well,
you know the rest.

46:20 As with the first half, Gillingham are straight into gear,
with Smith clean through, but Richard Edghill is alert to the
danger and slides in on the Gillingham man at the last moment.
He falls with arms flying but it is not a penalty. Replay is
showing us that the City man gets there fractionally ahead of
Smith and plays the ball onto his legs as he falls.

This Wembley pitch is really offering itself up for slide tackles,
it's fair to say. Ashby seems to be holding his face after a clash
with Shaun Goater too. Ashby actually played against City for

Watford in the 88-89 FA Youth Cup final. You will not be surprised to hear that there are no City players surviving that day ten years ago at the club today, such has been the vast turnover of playing- and non-playing staff in recent years.

49:00 Someone has just remarked that City were 12th in the 3rd division after defeat at York on 19th December. It has been quite a second half to the season to reach even this level. Gillingham were 6th that weekend by the way. Just 7,000 watched City's defeat at Bootham Cresent. That figure has also gone up by the small amount of 63,000 today. City's average this season, lest we forget, an unbelievable 28,000. I may mention that again later, depending on the stress levels that the club is putting us all through here.

50:00 We reach the fifty-minute mark and the rain is coming down in sheets again. Difficult to hold onto the ball, especially with tackles biting in at a fast rate, but the long ball must seem an even more enticing tactic now. Gillingham have the pace of Asaba to worry that big central defensive pair of Wiekens and Morrison, although Bob Taylor is not quite so quick off the mark.

53:00 CITY PRESSURE Two quick City corners in succession. Horlock dinks one left footed into the near post and the ball is rushed away from Wiekens and Crooks as they close in on it for a header. Wiekens looked to get in a back header but Crooks jumped with him and it may well have gone off the right back's head in the end. Referee Halsey gives a corner anyway. From the second one, it's Terry Cooke taking it right footed and Goater finally gets in on the act with a flashing header, which hits a defender and runs to safety. Goater didn't really get the direction right but he did connect properly at last. Lot of bodies in there jumping. Things livening up somewhat in the downpour.

54:00 Really greasy surface beginning to take its toll. Players slipping and miscontrolling the ball. Lot of aimless balls going into touch. Michael Brown personifies this with a shanked left wing cross that sails high over the bar.

Announcer gives us the attendance figure and it's a big one: 76,935, a record for this division and just below the top play-off figure ever, which was registered for Charlton v Sunderland in 1998.

57:00 First substitution: Galloway gives way to Mark Saunders, who has played here before, in the FA Vase final for Tiverton, believe it or not. Whether that fully prepares him for a match like this one is unclear.

58:00 Andy Hessenthaler is blocked by Lee Crooks through the middle as Gillingham's most industrious player again tries to shrug off the close midfield attention. The game is suddenly beginning to open up considerably, with the ball pinging end to end at the moment.

60:00 As if to confirm this, a City attack breaks down on the edge of the box and Gillingham quickly work the ball to midfield, where Smith hits an early through ball to try and put Bob Taylor in on goal. The ball is intercepted but the crowd are loving it now.

62:00 Sighter. Double miss by Shaun Goater. The big striker at last has a proper look in with two chances in a matter of seconds. He has been a peripheral figure so far and it shows with his finishing as his header is weak and is immediately followed by a wild swing with his right foot as the ball cannons back to him.

63:00 Danger for City. Again provided by Hessenthaler, who is clipped on the edge of the box by Wiekens, but he carries on past Michael Brown and smacks into Jeff Whitley. Referee Halsey has no hesitation in giving the free kick and it's Bob Taylor who attempts the curler, but to no effect. The ball sails wide of Weaver's far post.

64:00 Ch-ch-ch changes? Some activity down on the City bench with both Ian Bishop and Tony Vaughan warming up. Brave gamble by Joe Royle at this relatively early stage. I wonder who is coming off?

65:00 Double substitution City First change for City and it's the double one we expected. Andy Morrison, who is feeling a bad knee, is replaced by Tony Vaughan, whilst 34 year old Ian Bishop – birthday yesterday, incidentally – is also keen to get started in place of Michael Brown. Industry replaced by artistry for City.

67:00 Nearly the breakthrough That is so close to 1-0 for the Gills. They attack menacingly up the right flank, a long ball forward chased down by the willing running of Carl Asaba. He exchanges a clever one-two with Taylor and charges on before clipping the ball into the box. Richard Edghill's header is weak and drops right at the feet of Nicky Southall, whose oblique cross skids off Saunders' head and goes past the far post. The ball pings across the face of City's goal with Weaver rooted.

Gillingham have upped the tempo with a braver approach in the last few seconds. A goal feels imminent here.

69:15 Yellow card Bob Taylor the striker's trip on Jeff Whitley is pulled back by Mark Halsey. That's the second booking of the match and both have gone to Gillingham so far. City play on and Cooke's free kick hits a defender and runs for a corner. Ian Bishop collects and provides another dangerous cross, which is headed out this time by Barry Ashby. My word he has worked hard. Bishop and indeed Tony Vaughan too, have made an immediate impact for City here.

70:00 Really hotting up. Asaba is about to pull the trigger after being fed at the end of Smith's driving run, but Bishop of all people slides in with the saving tackle.

71:00 Oh so close Smith tires of the patient build up and whacks one from distance. It kicks up furiously on the wet turf as Weaver drops to make the save and the young keeper fumbles it. As it drops behind him he recovers to keep it off the line. Potentially horrible moment for Nicky Weaver.

73:00 This is getting increasingly chaotic now, as defenders slip in the difficult conditions. Now it's Bob Taylor thundering in but he is thwarted again.

74:00 Appeal for a penalty It's another weak one as Saunders goes sprawling. Tony Vaughan and Jeff Whitley both quick to snuff out the danger and no contact was made on Saunders as he surged through. Correct decision by Halsey.

75:10 Goater hits the post!!! There he is at last and how close City are to taking the lead. Gillingham pressure leads to City break out, with Richard Edghill playing it long to Dickov. The little Scot runs at the Gillingham defence, laying it off to Terry Cooke just as defenders are converging on him. Cooke delivers a killer cross to the far post, which Ashby should clear, but his boot misses it and it reaches Shaun Goater. With Dickov squealing for a cut back, Goater side foots it past Bartram and onto the post. It slaps back into play behind the goalkeeper and is cleared.

76:00 This is madness now as Gillingham are straight through at the other end with Taylor. There is a yawning space inviting the striker to run through. He cuts inside Tony Vaughan and angles a shot past Weaver and past the back post. Really open all of a sudden.

77:00 Oh. My. Word. Edghill misses his header, Weaver has to run out to collect the wayward ball and smacks it straight to Taylor mid territory. The striker needs no time to think and hits it straight towards the unguarded goal, but it drifts agonisingly wide with Weaver nowhere to be seen. Close to absolute disaster there for Royle's side.

80:00 Hard running Paul Dickov checks inside and as he prepares t move on, the ball clips his heels and falls instead to Terry Cooke. His left foot shot is tipped over the bar at full stretch by Bartram. It is quite amazing that this spell has not yet produced a goal.

82:00 What did I say. At last a GOAL!! And it goes to Gillingham. Gillingham 1-0 Manchester City. What a time to break through. Absolute madness at one end, disbelief at the other. Made by the running of Carl Asaba once again. He runs onto Smith's ball and makes a huge amount of ground. He is the one to collect the ball by the touchline, plays it into Smith and begins a long run in pursuit. As Smith holds it up, it's Asaba steaming past him as Smith releases it and the striker carries it into the box and attempts a kind of toe poke, which flies past Weaver into the top of the net. Half of Kent erupts behind that goal as Gillingham edge towards their goal of promotion to the first division.

83:00 And that is inches from clinching it Taylor reacts quickly to loose play by City by clipping an outrageous effort goalwards with his right foot. The ball is arrowing in when Weaver gets a slight hand to it and the ball nudges the far post and exits the field of play. Without the goalkeeper's tiny deflection that was going to be 2-0 and curtains for City. Nerve jangling stuff now.

84:00 Bartram keeps Dickov out. Best man versus superman. Dickov thought he had done it for City, reacting brilliantly to a low cross by Richard Edghill, but Bartram's instincts are just as sharp and he saves with his foot as the ball pings towards the goal. How terribly tough this must be for the City fans to take. They are staring another season in the third tier in the face now. Gillingham are poised to go up. Dickov is furious and wallops the ball against the advertising hoardings.

87:00 Goal!!! It's TWO for Gillingham!! City can pack up and go home. Gillingham 2-0 City Bob Taylor it is and how he deserves it for his afternoon's endeavour. His 21st goal of a fantastic season. He takes it on from Asaba's pass with Tony Vaughan in his wake and slots it home as calm as you like. Bye bye division two. Vaughan's face tells us all we need to know about City's dreadful predicament. All that effort just to stay down in this tough division for another year. **That's two goals in five minutes for Gillingham. City need two in three minutes to save themselves. Fantastic achievement from Tony Pulis and his men. The manager allows himself a little grin and there are hugs on the Gillingham bench. They've done it.**

88:00 Pulis reinforces immediately. Gillingham shutting up shop. Darren Carr replaces a visibly tired Carl Asaba, scorer of the first goal and provider of the second, to shore up the defensive lines. Sensible move with the clock ticking down remorselessly here. Some City fans are filing out but the majority stay open-mouthed with hands on heads. At the other end a loud rendition of "You're not singing anymore" cascades gleefully down towards the silent City fans. There's going to be a party in Kent tonight.

90:00 BUT WAIT! LATE HOPE FOR CITY. IT'S A GOAL FOR KEVIN HORLOCK. 2-1 now as City drag a modicum of respect into the afternoon. Horlock's daisy cutter comes after Dickov flicks Goater in. The big striker is blocked immediately and the ball runs free to the edge of the box, where Horlock sidefoots home as cool as you like. Surely much too little too late, but City have their consolation goal.

AND THERE WILL BE FIVE MINUTES OF ADDED TIME. THE CITY END ROARS ENCOURAGEMENT AS PULIS SHAKES HIS HEAD. WHERE HAS HALSEY FOUND FIVE MINUTES FROM?

90:00+3 Scrappy, desperate football now. Plenty of whistles coming up from the Gillingham end as the ball cannons around midfield.

90:00+5 Would you believe it?!!! CITY HAVE SCORED!!!! 2-2 in the fifth minute of added time. They've rescued it in the most dramatic way possible. Paul Dickov's the hero with a smashing right foot finish after the ball broke to him on the edge of the box. The little Scot let fly and it soared past Bartram and into the top corner. **The City end is a mass eruption of bodies, pulsing and cavorting. Amazing sights. Gillingham fans rooted to the spot. Incredible. Absolutely incredible!!!**

90:00+6 It's all over but in fact it isn't. 30 more minutes now and Gillingham have just taken off their top scorer. Tony Pulis has got the team talk of all team talks to deliver here. His Gillingham players look punch drunk after that. Pulis himself is effing and blinding to himself as the game ends.

Analysis: Never say never, if you follow Manchester City. Joe Royle's Cityitis has been turned on its head here as City replicate their neighbours' last minute heroics last week. Dickov, who has run and run all afternoon, deserves to be the centre of attention. A fine effort from the Scot, who came to City under Alan Ball's ill-fated reign. He has seen nothing other than chaos at City, and more of the same today, that's for sure. Surely City have the upper hand mentally now, after that. How do Gillingham pull themselves together?

Extra Time commences.

Strange atmosphere so far. It's scrappy, nervous and disjointed. Gillingham's players trying manfully to get their focus back on winning this game for a second time. City's, meanwhile, trying to calm themselves down after the euphoria of the great escape. Neither side able to put anything together. They look shattered both physically and mentally by what has transpired here.

Half time in Extra Time Manchester City 0-0 Gillingham

City prodding patiently, Gillingham walking in a daze. Good linking between Kevin Horlock and Paul Dickov down the left but it's all a little pedestrian after that scintillating final ten minutes of the ninety. City's bench contains the four wise men, Alex Stepney, Joe Royle, Willie Donachie and Asa Hartford. Four men sat alongside each other with such a wealth of experience.

You wonder what they can share with those players at this stage.

105:00 Substitution Gillingham. John Hodge replaces Mark Patterson

106:00 Yellow card Gerard Wiekens. City's second yellow, as the Dutchamn blocks the path of Nicky Southall. Nothing malicious or nasty, just the act of a man with tired legs and a numb brain.

108:30 Last flailings of this incredible match. Terry Cooke feeds the Goat but he doesn't score. Butters in quickly and bravely as Goater was about to shoot.

110:00 All City now as Ian Bishop slides Cooke in on the right, he fades inside a tackle and hits a left footer, which deflects for a corner. Corner taken quickly by Cooke, short to Bishop. He squares it intelligently to Jeff Whitley, whose shot is not clean but cannons up off Vaughan's head and just over the bar.

111:00 Loose at the City end. Weaver to the rescue, as Vaughan's slip sends the ball into the danger area, but the big City keeper punches it away from Hodge and then blocks a strange right footed follow up from Saunders, when it looked easier to hit it with his left.

112:00 Great Chance City Lot of action again now. Dickov heads Horlock's perfect cross into the arms of Vince Bartram, who hasn't put a glove wrong here today.

114:00 Big shout for a penalty to Gillingham!!! Halsey not interested. Saunders is away down the left, puts Hodge through at the edge of the box. He is closing in on Weaver and tries to cut the ball across the box but Whitley slides in on the ground and takes the ball out for a corner with his arm. That's 1-1 in penalties not given, one right at the start, the other right at the end.

120:00 last minute drama. Yellow or red for Carr, who has just run over Terry Cooke? Cooke had nutmegged Southall brilliantly but Carr just took him out. Halsey taking a long time to decide...but it's yellow in the end for a relieved Carr.

120:00+1 That is the last of the action. It will be penalties to decide this humdinger of a match. Both sets of players out on their feet. Mark Halsey decides the tunnel end will host the penalties and that is where all of City's noisy support is amassed. Will it make a difference? We are about to find out.

Penalty Shoot-out at Wembley. Mark Halsey strides up to the tunnel end goal to talk to Vince Bartram and Nicky Weaver. He has his tongue out. We know how he feels.

Long walk for Kevin Horlock, who will start the penalty competition. Great noise swelling up again as he places the spot kick looking extremely nervous. He was the player to miss the last time City were involved in a penalty shoot-out, last season in the League Cup at Blackpool.

Horlock scores! Manchester City 1-0 Gillingham Left footed, down the middle with Bartram diving the wrong way.

Mass of boos and jeering greets Paul Smith as he is the next to take the long walk. **Weaver saves with his feet!!! Gillingham a goal down. Manchester City 1-0 Gillingham** after two penalties.

Now it's Paul Dickov squaring up to his best mate Bartram. **Dickov hits both posts!!! Firm shot hits inside of left post,** travels along the line and comes bqack out off the other post. Amazing. Manchester City 1-0 Gillingham.

Adrian Pennock slams his spot kick wide!! Oh my word. This is not how to take penalties. **Manchester City 1-0 Gillingham, after 4 penalties.**

Terry Cooke is penalty taker number five. **And he scores.** Cooly slots into the side netting. Pefect penalty from the little winger. **Manchester City 2-0 Gillingham.**

John Hodge scores top corner for Gillingham. Super cool from the substitute with that wall of noise from the City fans in front of him. **Manchester City 2-1 Gillingham** after six pens.

Richard Edghill next up!! What is Joe Royle thinking? Edghill has never scored a first team goal for City, never mind a penalty. **Short run up and Edghill scores!!! In off the underside of the bar. Manchester City 3-1 Gillingham.**

Guy Butters is next. He has to score to keep Gillingham in it.

Weaver saves from Butters!!! It's all over CITY ARE PROMOTED 3-1 ON PENALTIES.

Incredible scenes here as the young goalkeeper embarks on a run that takes him past everyone. He doesn't know where he's going. He's just running and running in great big circles until he charges into Andy Morrison and that's where his gallop comes to an abrupt end, as you can imagine. A massive pile of City personnel in the centre circle now. What a way to do it. Ten turbulent years encapsulated in one afternoon's football for City. Quite extraordinary what has happened here today. This is a club that only knows how to do things the hard way, evidently. You can only imagine what it must feel like to support this lot.

Some immediate reactions amid the chaos:

First a very magnanimous Gills boss Tony Pulis: *"These games are usually pretty tight but it was very open today. City threw caution to the wind at two-down but they were the better team in extra time. Our lads are mentally drained..."*

Followed closely by an equally kind-hearted, if a little dishevelled Joe Royle: *"I feel sorry for Tony Pulis and his team. They're a terrific side, strong and hard to play against and they'll be back in the hunt again next season. But I still think the play-offs are a joker. You play 46 games then a cup competition. I never stopped believing, but it was tight, wasn't it? The nice thing is that today has finally ended Cityitis."*

Match-saver Paul Dickov: *"The worst thing about the penalty is I have sent Vince Bartram the wrong way. We'd been practising penalties in training since before the Wigan semi-final. It was sod's law that I couldn't replicate what I did in training because every single one was hitting the side netting. For it to hit both posts my heart just sank. It seemed to just sum up our day. We have been through every emotion."*

Richard Edghill, who chose today to net his first ever City goal from the penalty spot: *"I didn't mean to go that close to the bar! I'd practised the same way every time and it had always gone roughly up the middle of the goal. I think nerves played a big part in it. I put the ball down and stepped back and that was when I started to feel really nervous. Luckily it went in."*

Does he really think that? So, City have done it. There isn't a dry eye in the house or down Wembley Way, where people are wandering around like zombies. Totally and utterly drained from what they have experienced here today. As the manager of another football team might say, "Football, bloody hell."

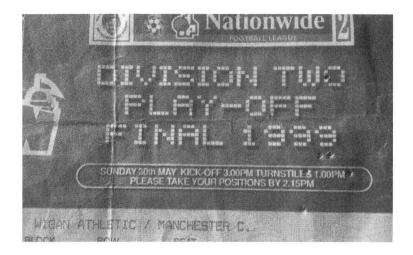

**FA Cup 4th round replay. Tottenham v Manchester City
Wednesday 4th February 2004**

**"Squeezed it to Tarnat. There was a bit of tugging on Macken.
He's scored!!! Jon Macken!"**

A tale of two managers tonight at White Hart Lane: "*I fear the
chop!*" said City boss Kevin Keegan not two weeks ago, after his
stuttering side was plunged into relegation chaos. A 1-1 draw at
home to Blackburn Rovers meant Keegan's charges had gone 11
games without a win. Now you can make that 12 after last
week's defeat at Highbury, plus a draw in the FA Cup, with that
1-1 result at the City of Manchester Stadium last weekend with
tonight's opponents Tottenham Hotspur.

In total it's one win out of the last 18 for City.

"*We have got to learn the key to winning,*" Keegan says and
tonight, if his City side once again fails to find the key to the
door, they will be well and truly locked out of this year's FA Cup
competition.

Meanwhile **could it be Mancini to Spurs?** Newspaper reports
continue to link Tottenham to Italian Roberto Mancini and the
Lazio boss has stated he is still thinking over an offer to take
over in North London. This comes in the wake of speculation
that Giovanni Trappatoni has already shaken hands on a
contract at White Hart Lane beginning straight after Euro 2004,
where he will lead the Italian national side for one last time.
Mancini meanwhile has said this: "Yes I spoke to them. I have
always said that I would like to train an English club as the
football there is so enjoyable". What an enticing prospect that
would be to see a coach of Mancini's standing manage in
England.

The first game of this 4th round tie was a drab affair that followed a familiar path for City. Some degree of hope delivered with the opening goal, then an obvious failure to capitalise on the lead, then disaster and recriminations as Spurs came back into it and got their equaliser.

Part of the after-match heat arose because of the way City conceded the Spurs goal, a simple cross that was missed by the goalkeeper, and that also brings us round immediately to tonight's hot topic: the men who guard the goals. City's season has been beset with problems between the posts. Starting the season with the ultra-experienced David Seaman, all seemed secure, but the former Arsenal and England man's form was so poor, he has decided to retire, leaving City in a bit of a fix. David James is newly arrived and is set to become City's number one, but alas he is cup-tied for tonight's game and cannot play. With Nicky Weaver injured and last weekend's custodian Kevin Stuur Ellegaard's confidence in tatters, we wait to see what manager Keegan's final solution to this evening's problem will be.

Someone Keegan will certainly be relying on is 16-goal top scorer Nicolas Anelka, current run eight in eight games, who says: "The situation is a little bit odd for me, because I have been pleased with the way I have been playing. Since the beginning of the season I have scored 16 goals. I have never done that before. I feel that I am a better player than I was two years ago, my game has changed and I put that down to working with Kevin. I don't think he has any desire to leave the club at all..."

Anelka's every move and every quote is being assiduously scrutinised by the great and good of the press at the moment of course, after he intimated that he might want out and how much he admired Manchester United, not the soft words guaranteed to get you a free fish supper in the City supporting homelands.

We await team news and expect to be able to share it with you in a few short minutes. Just across town we also have Fulham and Everton fighting it out for the right to play West Ham next, but Telford and Millwall is off due to a waterlogged pitch.

19:00 In the meantime, let us look at these great clubs' record in the FA Cup for a moment, shall we? Spurs won the Cup six times in the 30 year period between 1961 and 1991 but have not won it since. That makes it twelve years since they last carried off the Cup, a period comprising four semi-final defeats. City, meanwhile, haven't had a sniff of this silverware since 1969, a brief break from winning things of just 34 years, as the ticker at Old Trafford so judiciously reminds us. The last time the club got to the final, they lost in a replay (the first of its kind at a Wembley Cup Final) to... Tottenham Hotspur.

No need to mention Ricky Villa just now, though.

Spurs' loss to Coventry in the 1987 final was whilst under the stewardship of present caretaker boss David Pleat, whom City have further reason to fear, as he was the man in charge of Luton Town in 1983, when the Hatters dumped City into the second division. Football's swings and roundabouts! Expect a few wide eyed stares from City if Pleat shows up in a fawn suit tonight.

19:05 The prize for tonight's replay winners is of course already known after the 4th round games from ten days ago. The winners will travel to Manchester United, 3-0 winners at Northampton last time out. Not exactly what either side this evening would have wanted, but extra incentive for City to climb into what would be a gripping Manchester derby in the 5th round.

The weekend fixtures were also unkind to both sides. Spurs were given an away London derby to deal with on Saturday and lost it 2-1 at Craven Cottage to 7th placed Fulham. City, meanwhile, only played on Sunday, losing controversially at Highbury to leaders Arsenal and having Nicolas Anelka sent off. Anelka and City were particularly aggrieved at referee Alan Wiley's interpretation of their bout of push and shove over the ball after Anelka's goal, as Ashley Cole did not receive the same punishment as the City striker for taking part in the same incident. Anelka will miss any 6th round tie, but that is already taking things a little far, as there is the small matter of tonight's game and a possible 5th round tie at Old Trafford to circumnavigate first.

There has not been much time for either side to recuperate for this one then.

19:10 Very interesting team news just in. Big gamble from Kevin Keegan. City's goalkeeping problems will be handed over on a silver platter to debutant Icelander Arni Gautur Arason, 28 years old, and the ex-Rosenburg shot stopper. Arason joined the club just before the drawn first game between the sides in Manchester on 24th January. He has 33 caps for Iceland but can he do it on a damp night on Tottenham High Road? We will shortly find out. Keegan, ever the gambler, rolls the dice once again.

City line up like this then: **Arason: Sun Jihai, Dunne, Distin, Tarnat; Wright-Philips, Barton, Bosvelt, Sinclair; Anelka, Fowler.**

Tottenham will look like this: **Keller: Carr, Richards, Gardner, Ziege; Dalmat, King, Brown, Davies; Postiga, Keane.**

City's new loan recruit from Olympique de Marseille, Daniel van Buyten, has not made the cut, as he signed too late to be registered for this tie. David Sommeil headed south as part of a complicated swap loan deal. Likewise Spurs' scorer in the first tie, Gary Docherty misses out tonight and is replaced by Dean Richards at the back.

19:25 Keegan and City will have mixed feelings on seeing Helder Postiga start. Maybe Spurs fans won't be overwhelmed themselves. The low-scoring Portuguese did find the net in the Carling Cup match between the sides back in November, however. This was a game that Robbie Fowler also scored in and he returns for City tonight after a bout of flu at the weekend.

So tonight Spurs attempt to knock City out of both domestic cup competitions in one season, a feat managed by Middlesbrough against City only ten years ago.

Spurs are in good form at home, having smashed five past Wolves and four against Birmingham, as well as a hard fought 2-1 win over Liverpool. Their home form has been pretty strong, therefore, and City's attempts away from the City of Manchester Stadium have been, let's say, patchy.

19:40 We're all set. Players are down in the cramped White Hart Lane tunnel and the ground has filled up nicely. Spurs officials were expecting a turn-out of around 30,000 tonight and City have sold a fraction under 2,000 to their supporters. It's a long way to come on a wintry Wednesday night, but optimism amongst football supporters is always the last flame to die out. Referee is Mr Rob Styles.

19:42 Jermain Defoe, Spurs new £8 million pounds signing from West Ham is walking out onto the pitch to receive the acclaim of the crowd. He can't play tonight but is guest of honour at the club that he hopes to score a hatful of goals for. Warm welcome for him.

19:45 We're off, City get us under way and the ball is pinging around like a hot potato. The home side looking very perky. Bright start from Spurs with passes flashing between white shirts.

02:00 AND BANG, WHAT DID I SAY? Tottenham score with their first proper attack of the match! New 'keeper Arni Arason's first touch of the ball as a Manchester City player is to scoop it out of the back of his net after just two minutes of his debut. Does anyone know what the Icelandic for *"Typical City"* is? Stephane Dalmat with the ball in across the box to Ledley King, who turns Michael Tarnat inside out, ignores the first opening to shoot and then thrashes his shot into the top corner. That was a finish any of Spurs' strikers would have been proud of. King's first of the season. He's obviously been saving that up. What a start for Spurs and White Hart Lane is rocking as the home fans can already see a big cup tie at Old Trafford approaching on the horizon. **TOTTENHAM 1-0 MANCHESTER CITY.**

05:00 Penalty appeal! City's first meaningful sortie and it ends with confusion and an appeal for a penalty. Anthony Gardner was hesitant, leaving a loose ball to Keller and Sun Jihai very nearly nipped in to score. The Chinaman ends up on the floor as his legs get tangled with Casey Keller. His legs go up and some City arms go up too, but Mr Styles is not interested.

06:00 Early substitution for Tottenham. Helder Postiga cannot carry on and is replaced by Gus Poyet, who was sent off v Crystal Palace in the 3rd round. Early reshape for the home side.

16:00 Poor header out by Anthony Gardner, who is having a jittery start out there, falls perfectly for Robbie Fowler who lashes a left foot shot inches wide of Keller's left hand post. Close call that one.

18:00 City straight through again, as Fowler burst through the inside left channel, eases himself past Richards, takes aim and squirts a low shot past Keller but also just past the far post. Good reaction to going a goal down so early from City, this.

19:00 What a kick in the teeth for City. Goal for Tottenham! Just as City were beginning to look really menacing going forward, those two good chances for Fowler in particular, it's Spurs who score out of nothing. Majestic flighted ball from Steven Carr from inside his own half lands at Robbie Keane's feet. Those twinkling feet are too much for Distin, who is on the wrong side of the Spurs man, and Dunne who seems to be coming in backwards for some reason. Keane – cool as you like – flicks the ball past Arason with the outside of his left boot and Sun Jihai can do nothing on the line. **TOTTENHAM 2-0 MANCHESTER CITY**. One foot in the next round.

27:00 Going from bad to worse for City, as Nicolas Anelka walks casually off the pitch holding his groin. Has a short word with Juan Carlos Osario about his condition and walks off down the tunnel. Certainly in more of a hurry to leave the pitch than he was at Highbury on Sunday when he was shown the red card. No dallying this time from Monsieur Anelka and Jon Macken is having to rip his gear off quickly to get onto the pitch and restore City's numbers.

28:00 Macken straight in to the action, freeing Wright Phillips down the wing with a beautifully weighted pass. The little winger cuts the ball back but Fowler gets his legs in a tangle and produces what is little more than an air shot with his suspect right foot.

37:00 Unbelievable. GOAL SPURS. Spurs have another! Surely they are now through to face Manchester United in the next round. If they lose this one they'll want shooting. Ball runs to Michael Brown, who is hacked continually by a frustrated Joey Barton. The youngster was far too eager. Christian Ziege lines it up, waits, then curls an expert free kick over the wall and back down in to the net. Arason flying like a falling wardrobe misses the save as the ball goes past and over him. But it wasn't out of his reach. Just to round off a rich night for City, Barton was also booked for that crude bit of defending. **SPURS 3-0 CITY**. Call for the fire brigade.

Kevin Keegan is an awful grey colour and is standing stock still on the touchline.

HALF TIME: TOTTENHAM 3-0 MANCHESTER CITY. From bad to worse. It looks very much like it's a **RED CARD.** Joey Barton, as the teams are walking off, still has a word or two to share with Mr Styles and he doesn't appear to take kindly to them. We'll have confirmation for you just as soon as we have it, but it looks very much like City's second half will begin with ten men, three goals down and without top scorer Anelka, injured and in the dressing room.

Confirmation from Mr Styles that Barton received a second yellow card after the half time whistle for abusive language. Well, well. There's always the league to concentrate on, City.

So, what does Kevin Keegan have to do in that half time dressing room? There's the small matter of getting the side reorganised with a midfielder less. Then he will want to pep up the strikers with some *bons mots* now that Anelka is off injured. Oh, yes, and he might want to have a quick word about how they are going to need four second half goals to drag themselves out of a sticky situation here at White Hart Lane. When I say sticky, I mean sticky.

For Spurs, more of the same would be great, but I would guess David Pleat will be preaching a steady start to the second period and to keep City at bay, then pick them off as they inevitably tire. The home fans, meanwhile, can start making travel arrangements for a trip north to Old Trafford in the 5th round.

Second half is about to start. Could this be Mr Keegan's last 45 minutes in charge of Manchester City?

47:00 WHAT A START TO THE SECOND HALF. GOAL to City! Tottenham 3-1 Manchester City. Just like we had in the 1st half, so the 2nd starts with a goal too and it's just what David Pleat will have been warning his men against. Wright Phillips is upended in a central position near the edge of the box. Michael Tarnat runs up and, instead of one of his trademark howitzers, he dinks a delicate little chip with the outside of his left foot. Stephane Dalmat has gone to sleep on the far post and Distin crashes past him and plants a scruffy header past Keller, with his legs flying as he tries to keep his balance. Well, at least that looks a little more respectable for City.

50:00 So close to 4-1. Wonder save from Arason! In fact that's the double save of the season, looking at it again. Robbie Keane chopped down by Distin. Ziege again steps up to try and repeat the first half magic. His free kick is another beauty, and even takes a slight deflection, but Arason somehow arches his back to tip it up onto the bar. The ball bounces out to Poyet not six yards out, who nods it in for 4... but no, Arason, as quick as a cobra, is back off the ground to pounce on the ball as it bounces on the line. An absolutely stunning save from the debutant.

60:00 Wow, City go from respectable to back in the match! Incredible scenes here as City make it 3-2. Good pressure from the ten men, starting and ending with Paul Bosvelt. The ball breaks to the Dutchman, who bangs it into the ground and up off Gardner's back into the net. The ball just loops slowly, apologetically away from Casey Keller, who had gone the other way. My word, what a match we have here now. Spurs looking a bit shocked, as you would imagine. **TOTTENHAM 3-2 MANCHESTER CITY.**

70:00 Two great chances for Poyet in a minute. Keane jabs it through to the Uruguayan, who turns on a peso and whacks his shot just past Arason's right hand post. Straight afterwards, Poyet is fouled by Distin. Freekick is fired in and the same player produces a text book header which Arason somehow tips around the base of the post. Elastic arms from the Icelander.

79:00 Oh. My. God. IT'S THREE-THREE. City equaliser through Shaun Wright Phillips! This is utter and total madness. Hint of offside about it too, as Fowler slips the winger through in the inside right channel (not for the first time this evening). Wright Phillips keeps his cool, scampers after it, reaching the ball just before the onrushing Keller and lifting it expertly over the American. It take an absolute age to drop, but when it does, it goes inside the far post. One of the best cup comebacks in recent history has been carried out here by City. Amazing stuff.

Truly amazing. If any City fans left at half time, they'll be getting some interesting score updates on their mobiles about now.

80:00 Keegan still looks grey in the face. I guess we all do. There are increasing numbers of Spurs fans, who looks a little green around the gills too. Incredible climax here. This is what the FA Cup is all about, I would say.

85:00 Just five to go here now, as Robbie Keane miskicks close in. Spurs still providing sporadic attacks but they all look a little numb to have thrown this away to ten-man City, to be frank. They will be looking to come again more strongly in extra time, when their one man advantage is sure to begin to tell. Mind you I was saying that at half time.

90:00 Edging in to time added on now. What a comeback from City. Now for extratime.

90:00+1 OR NOT! OR NOT!! WHAT ONE MAN ADVANTAGE? CITY HAVE WON IT!!!!! 4-3 TO MANCHESTER CITY AND THE COMEBACK OF ALL COMEBACKS IS COMPLETE. THE GREATEST FA CUP COMEBACK IN HISTORY, ladies and gentleman. I – and all 30, 400 here tonight, cannot believe my eyes. SPURS 3-4 CITY in the 91st minute of this pulsating, unbelievable, ridiculous game. It's Jon Macken getting a towering head on Michael Tarnat's deep cross from the left touchline. Sun Jihai works it to Sibierski, whose last act as he falls under pressure is to squirt it out to Tarnat. First time cross, with Jackson sliding to the floor and King beaten in the air at the back post. Macken rises like a salmon and angles the ball back across Keller and into the far corner. Amazing and it's the one player who could have put the first tie to bed but fluffed his lines. A script that Agatha Christie would have turned away as completely preposterous.

You can say you were there. You can say you saw it with your own eyes, but you will still not be able to believe it. Ten against eleven? No worries? Top scorer off injured? That's ok. Three-nil down at half time? We'll take that. One win in 18? Yep, that's us too. Manchester City, the gift that keeps on giving, have exploded all the certainties football has ever given us here and will take their place proudly in the 5th round of the FA Cup.

90:00+2 Incredibly the game is still going on, would you believe it. Hardly anyone has noticed! Nobody dare watch. Bosvelt wellies it away. Distin wellies it away. Wright Phillips wellies it away. **And Rob Styles blows his whistle on a historic night of FA Cup football. City have done it!! They win this replay 4-3 with one of the most outrageous displays I have ever witnessed.**

Spare a quick thought for Tottenham. How on earth do you pick yourself up after that?

Just while out attention was taken ever so slightly by that second half at White Hart Lane, Fulham were also booking a berth in the 5th round, by beating Everton 2-1. They will now be at home to West ham in the 5th round. Revised draw looks like this:

Man Utd v Man City
Tranmere v Swansea
Telford/Millwall v Burnley
Sunderland v Birmingham
Fulham v West Ham
Arsenal v Chelsea
Liverpool v Portsmouth
Sheffield Utd v Colchester

2145 Quick word with the two managers. This ought to be good:

Kevin Keegan: "Long after we're all dead, six foot under or cremated or whatever we choose to do with ourselves, they'll be talking about this game, showing this match to say what the FA Cup's all about."

"I said to Faz at half time, "Where's the nearest job centre?" We were that bad to be quite honest. But they've kept me in a job second half. Leave the job centre, get back up, back to work, eh?"

With that the little man leaves and is swallowed by a crowd of bodies in the tunnel. What a night he's had. The full gamut of emotions and you have to say he looks absolutely drained, bless him.

David Pleat: "They've let themselves down here tonight, they've let the supporters down. What I need to see now is a reaction. I can change some of the players that were playing here tonight".

Well, will we ever know exactly what was said in that Manchester City dressing room at half time? What did Keegan come up with to inspire that performance from his players? We leave you with this classic exchange between Sky reporter Rob Hawthorn and David Pleat down in the tunnel just now:

Pleat: "That's what makes football the game it is: utterly unpredictable..."
Hawthorn: "Understatement of the year that, David..."
Pleat: "Thank you." (Exits stage left).

What theatre indeed. We have been royally entertained here by two clubs trying to live up to that FA Cup final replay nearly 25 years ago. I think they may have just put that little one to bed here tonight with what they have served up for us.

Manchester City 1 Manchester United 0. FA Cup Semi-Final. 16th April, 2011.

"As soon as he went past Vidic, you knew what was coming."

4:00 pm. Welcome to Wembley, and a semi-final that ticks all the boxes, with a fascinating duel on the way between the two Manchester clubs, a chance perhaps for City to announce their arrival at the top table once and for all.

This is City's first Wembley visit since their infamous 1999 play-off final appearance, and they beat Reading to get here, knowing their opponents just prior to kick-off. So while this is City's 11th semi-final, it's their first for 30 years. Let's hope for their sake it was worth the wait. During that time there have been near-misses, false hope galore and many a broken dream. Finally they are in a position to usher in a period of sustained success. In their way though stands a formidable foe.

And let's look at some of the clubs that have reached a semi-final since City last did. Wimbledon, Coventry, Portsmouth, Brighton, Chesterfield, Oldham Athletic, Luton town and many more.

4:05 pm. The pitch and the stands look as pristine and alluring as ever as the first few fans arrive to take in the occasion. No problem with the playing conditions or the weather today, which should make for a great game.

4:15 pm. An hour to go and that can only mean one thing – the team sheets are out.

City's team: Hart, Kompany, Zabaleta, Lescott, Kolarov, Johnson, Barry, Silva, De Jong, Toure & Balotelli.

<u>United's team</u>: Van Der Sar, Ferdinand, Vidic, Evra, O'Shea, Park, Carrick, Nani, Valencia, Scholes, Berbatov.

Much of the build-up to the game has focused on the absence of two strikers, with both sides set to be without their most talismanic attacking weapons. Carlos Tevez is out with a hamstring injury picked up at Anfield, whilst United must do without Wayne Rooney, serving a domestic ban after the rather bizarre controversy created by him screaming into a camera at Upton Park post-goal. We're all a bit bemused over that one. Still, he won't be doing that again.

Alex Ferguson watches from the stands, due to a domestic touchline ban. Naughty boy. It's a record five match ban too, after Ferguson criticised Martin Atkinson following a defeat to Chelsea recently. His absence won't help United, but his team enter the game on the back of seven consecutive victories, so start the contest as favourites.

And as you would expect, United's PR campaign has been in full flow this week, and Paul Scholes has commented on how City are not United's main rivals just yet.

"When they are fourth or fifth, I don't think they can be classed as a main rival," said Scholes. "Our main rivals are obviously Arsenal and Chelsea. I think City are just a rival because of where they are and Liverpool the same."

Let's hope for his sake his comments don't come back to bite him on his behind. For the record, City are 4th, and their form isn't great, a thrashing of Sunderland sandwiched between defeats to Chelsea and Liverpool, though you get the feeling their minds were elsewhere at Anfield on Monday, where they were 3-0 down by half-time. United however are coming off the back of three league wins, and look good for yet another title.

4:50pm. Meanwhile, in the build up to the game, Alex Ferguson has admitted that playing the game at Wembley might have a physical effect on his team.

"It can drain the players," he said. "There is an impact in terms of the emotional build-up to the game. The fact it is at Wembley makes it more of an occasion, simply because of the name. "Obviously it is a different stadium now. Those Twin Towers were a landmark and I wouldn't think the pitch is as tiring as the old Wembley because they have changed it so many times. It is a derby game in London, which is unusual but we are ready for it. We have got the momentum at the moment. We are winning games, which is important at this time of the season. The consistency of the team has been good and we are playing well. Our players have a great determination. I am really pleased with that. It has given us a good chance."

4:55 pm. The referee for today's game is Mike Dean, who is busy with his team doing all the required pre-game checks.

5:00 pm. Today is the 159th time that the red and blue halves of Manchester have faced each other but amazingly the first time that they have done so at Wembley. United are ahead with 66 victories against City's 42 and there have been 50 draws.

The route to Wembley: It has hardly been the smoothest journey to Wembley for City. It started with a 2-2 draw at Leicester in the 3rd round, before winning the replay 4-2. Then it looked for a while as if they would be subject to a giant-killing from Notts County until an Edin Dzeko equalizer ensured a replay that they cruised to victory in, 5-0. The 5th round was more straightforward, with a routine 3-0 win over Aston Villa, and finally, with the knowledge that United awaited, City beat Reading 1-0 to ensure today's intriguing fixture.

For United, their toughest test came early on, with a 1-0 win over fierce rivals Liverpool at Old Trafford. They then won 2-1 at Southampton, stumbled past Crawley Town 1-0, before defeating Arsenal 2-0 in the quarter finals. It's not been the easiest of runs, so they should come to Wembley full of confidence.

From 759 clubs to just 4 – it's semi-final day.

5:10 pm. Sorry to start the action with a moan, but – it's very helpful to have the semi-final at Wembley today, with such a huge demand for tickets. But it is still wrong. Reaching Wembley is about the blue riband event of a tournament (the final, of course), and to use the venue for the semi-finals as well just takes away from the main event. Tomorrow Stoke and Bolton will play here and there will be a big demand for tickets, but will it be full? I doubt it – and two teams from the north would have been better served making a short trip to Old Trafford, the Etihad or somewhere else suitable for the occasion. Still, there's a £900m stadium to be paid off, so this is how it will always be now.

Rant over. On with the football.

5:15 pm. It seems City fans are more up for this occasion, as they seem to be filling up their sections earlier than their red neighbours. United fans will note a Wembley visit is nothing out of the ordinary for them, but without FA Cup success for 7 years now, they could do with a win just as much as City.

5:20 pm. And on cue, as the United line-up is read out over the tannoy, City fans turn their backs en masse and perform the Poznan, a celebration borrowed from the fans of......no.......hang on.......sorry, it's gone, I can't remember.

Despite my earlier rant, it's always great to see two teams come out of the Wembley tunnel and a stadium of this size split into two colours. And here come those teams, as kick-off approaches. Only one of the managers is allowed near the pitch of course on this occasion.

There were 33,000 tickets allocated to each side, so no surprise to see Wembley full to the rafters, as both Manchester clubs aim to return here for the final on 14th May. The corporate sections are the slowest to fill, as per usual. Those free bars don't drink themselves.

All the pleasantries are done, it's time for battle.

5:30 pm. **Here we go, the 1st of this season's FA Cup semi-finals kicks off.**

05:00: Little early action, as the two teams size each other up. Plenty of noise from the crowd, though, as both sets of fans engage in some friendly banter.

10:55: It has been a quiet start from both sides, as they settle into the match, and the first shot is a tame effort wide from Adam Johnson. The only other incident of note was Nani getting an accidental foot in his mouth from Nigel De Jong. The boy who cried wolf got little sympathy not surprisingly.

14:00: **BERBATOV SHOULD SCORE**. The first big chance of the match and United should be ahead. Twice. Berbatov manages to kiss two golden opportunities within 30 seconds. First, some great link up play sees Park release Berbatov on goal, but his shot is well saved from Hart. Then almost immediately a superb Nani turn sees him free and he squares the ball to Berbatov who somehow manages to spoon the ball over the bar when it was easier to score from just a few yards out. Berbatov picks up a knock to his ankle for good measure.

24:00: Vidic loses his marker at a corner but glances the ball wide.

31:30: **BARRY INCHES AWAY.** The first half-chance to City. Silva weaves his magic on the right and puts a cross in that falls to Barry, but on the turn he can only put a fierce shot into the side-netting.

33:30: Balotelli takes aim from 30 yards out and Van Der Sar is forced to tip the ball over the bar.

35:40: Half chance for Lescott who creeps round the back of United's defence at a corner but blazes over.

42:00: City have certainly improved with time. Yaya Toure puts on a turbo charge but his shot is deflected wide by Vidic. From the resulting corner it comes to Kompany 30 yards out, and a rare shot from him has real venom but flashed wide.

45:00+2: And that's half-time.

HALF-TIME – MANCHESTER CITY 0 MANCHESTER UNITED 0.

So it's stalemate at Wembley as the two Manchester sides walk off the pitch. It was a half of two halves, United stronger in the early minutes, and they should have gone ahead through Berbatov. But City grew into the match and ended the half stronger, which should make for a fascinating second half.

Both managers will be fairly happy you'd imagine at the break, so don't expect any changes to the sides just yet. The key will be who starts the second half strongest.

Almost ready to go in the second half, and the corporate sections are depressingly empty still. It really doesn't help this shiny new stadium when there are swathes of empty seats in a central positions when the game is in progress. Sorry, I'm moaning again.

SECOND HALF KICKS OFF – MANCHESTER CITY 0 MANCHESTER UNITED 0.

48:00: Quiet start to the half again, as both teams look to keep the ball.

51:50: GOAL! Manchester City 1 Manchester united 0. And it is the blue half of Manchester celebrating as United hand them a goal on a plate out of nowhere. A sliced clearance from Van Der Sar goes straight to Silva, United dispossess him, but then Carrick passes straight to Yaya Toure who surges into the area and slots home through the legs of Van Der Sar. A disastrous and costly mistake from Carrick.

The City fans in the stadium are ecstatic, and Poznans are breaking out sporadically. United have it all to do now, and their influence has waned after the early stages. You feel they need something different to turn this around, and a few of their substitutes are sent down the touchline to warm up.

57:00: City snapping into tackles now and dominating possession. The goal has changed the whole complex of the match.

61:00: Toure surges forward and releases Balotelli, but a poor 1st touch prevents a clear opening and Vidic gets the tackle in and concedes a corner.

61:30: From the resulting corner, Johnson sees his cross deflected behind by Van Der Sar. City well on top here.

62:30: Lescott glances a header wide from a Silva cross when he should have done better. Berbatov half asleep there and wasn't watching his man.

65:00: Manchester United substitution – Hernandez is on for Valencia.

65:30: United have a free kick in a dangerous position after Zabaleta fouls Park. Zabaleta is booked. Nani steps up, and his shot cannons back off the bar. The replay shows a deflection off the head of Balotelli and Hart thus does well to tip it onto the woodwork.

67:00: Mario Balotelli picks up his customary yellow card for a foul.

71:00. RED CARD for Paul Scholes. Is that United's chance gone? Paul Scholes goes in high and late on Pablo Zabaleta and can have no complaints at being dismissed. Scholes catches Zabaleta on his hip and he knew what was coming. A total lack of discipline from a frustrated Scholes, and United are up against it now.

73:10: Substitution -Oliveira Anderson coming on for Dimitar Berbatov, as Alex Ferguson tries to shake things up and offer something different as an attacking force.

73:57: Booking for Nigel De Jong for a crude foul. De Jong doing what he does best there, but City will profit from keeping a man advantage.

76:50: United need a spark here, they have stuttered their way through the first three quarters of this game, who is going to be the hero and rescue the tie? Certainly won't be Michael Carrick who has just curled a very tame effort from the edge of the box into Hart's grateful hands.

78:12: Adam Johnson's afternoon is over, he's replaced by Shaun Wright-Phillips.

80:21: A shot from Ji-Sung Park, but it doesn't trouble Joe Hart, and United are seeing plenty of the ball, but not offering a great threat at the moment.

81:00: Half a chance for Hernandez - who has barely had a kick since coming on - but the Mexican's shot from 10 yards was blocked out by a melee of blue shirts.

81:47: Shaun Wright-Phillips sends in a cross, saved by Edwin Van der Sar. Routine for the keeper.

83:12: Substitution. John O'Shea goes off and Fabio Da Silva comes on.

83:47: Patrice Evra has an effort at goal from just inside the box that misses to the right of the goal.

84:30: Vincent Kompany goes into the book for what would be termed unsporting behaviour- he'll take that, as the clock ticks down further. For unsporting behaviour, I mean a deliberate foul.

86:00: The game is very stretched now, United throwing huge numbers of bodies forward, but to no avail (yet). Is there a sting in the tail of this game? As I type, there is a final change for City: David Silva is replaced by Patrick Vieira.

87:00: No, it's not happening for United. One section of reds fans celebrate but Nani's shot rippled into the side netting. Then Patrice Evra produces a drilled left-footed shot from deep inside the penalty box which goes wide of the left-hand upright.

89:00: Toure has the chance to wrap it up, but he can't get the ball out of his feet in the box and Van der Sar (just about) manages to block and clear. That was a real chance, but it should be too late to come back and haunt City.

90:00: Andy Townsend compares Toure's performance to that of a "galloping stallion". That's one way of putting it I guess. Whatever your choice of flowery language, he's certainly made a difference today.

92:43: Mario Balotelli takes a shot from 35 yards out, but that was always clearing the bar. Nice bit of time-wasting though as the ball disappears in the crowd.

95:06: Fabio Da Silva challenges Aleksandar Kolarov unfairly and gives away a free kick. Joe Hart takes the direct free kick, slowly. Surely that is it now, and with that foul goes United's chances to take this match to extra-time.

95:38. Full-time. Manchester City 1 Manchester United 0. And that is it! Mike Dean blows for the end of the match, and City are victorious.

And joy aplenty for City's players and fans alike as half the crowd evacuates the stadium. Ah well, they should be home within the hour. After early domination from United, this was a fair result, City growing into the game as it progressed, and they were clearly the better side in the 2nd half. The red card for Paul Scholes effectively ended United's challenge.

And whilst the game may be over, the pitch action isn't. Mario Balotelli does what Mario Balotelli does best, and appears to have wound up a couple of the United players, most notably Anderson and a rather vexed Rio Ferdinand. Anderson grabs his shirt, and Ferdinand is in his face, but as you would expect, Mario is not overly bothered. And who can blame him? Deep in the action though is Roberto Mancini, who does his best to separate the players. Spoilsport.

It seems Mr Balotelli was brandishing his City badge in the direction of the United fans – well the few that remained anyway.

7:30 pm. So it's a wonderful day for the blue half of Manchester, and City now wait to see who they will play in the final as Stoke City and Bolton Wanderers battle it out tomorrow. Whoever they meet, City must surely be confident of lifting their first trophy in a generation, having overcome their fiercest rivals.

7:40pm. Roberto Mancini has spoken after the game, and naturally seems quite pleased with his day's work.
"I am very happy for our supporters, because they deserve this. It is important to start winning trophies, and I stand by my claim that if we win the FA Cup this year we can try for the title next season. This could be a turning point for us, but it is important to remember there is another game to win. I think we can go on from this to win the FA Cup and secure a top-four finish."

No such words of optimism from Alex Ferguson – in fact no words at all, the Scot taking defeat with his usual grace. With no poor refereeing decisions to blame, there was probably little point him saying anything anyway. We're hearing though that Mancini's overrunning press conference made him do a swift U-turn back to the dressing room.

7:50pm. A few more words instead from his Italian counterpart. "It's difficult to play against United. They're used to playing this type of game every year. For us, it was the first time after a long time," said Mancini.

"Maybe we had some fear in the first 20-25 minutes. In the last 10, 15 minutes of the first half, we started to play high, we started to press.

"In the second half, we dominated the game. I am happy because we had fantastic spirit and we beat a team like United." And a diplomatic answer from Mancini on the small fracas involving Mario Balotelli after full-time, which Mancini amazingly didn't even though I recall him separating the players.

"I didn't see it. I want to wait because every time, 'It's Balotelli's fault'," said Mancini. "We can put him in jail? Next week, we can put him in jail for this."

8:00pm. And that is that. City are in the final and are the clear favourites to win this year's FA Cup. Only Bolton Wanderers or Stoke City stand in their way now. Tune in tomorrow to see who that will be, and once more, congratulations to the blue half of Manchester, many of whom will have a fun journey back north tonight.

Manchester United 1 Manchester City 6 – 23rd October 2011.

'It was our worst ever day. It's the worst result in my history, ever. Even as a player I don't think I ever lost 6-1. I can't believe the scoreline.'

12:15 pm. A hearty welcome and a good afternoon from Old Trafford, where the top two, and most of Manchester, will do battle.
Is this a sign of things to come, the two clubs fighting for the top spot? Possibly, and on this occasion, it's the visitors that travel across the city with a two point lead at the top, so they have a good chance to put some daylight between themselves and the rest today as the reigning champions meet the noisy neighbours.
There's always a sense of expectation on derby day, and this could be a cracker. In fact, we almost guarantee it (or your money back).

City won late in the Champions League in the week against Villareal, and the goal hero from that game Sergio Aguero is expected to start, as is Wayne Rooney, who helped himself to two goals in the week against CS Otelul Galati. Could one of these two be pivotal today?

12:30 pm. And their inclusion is confirmed, as the team news filters in with an hour until kick-off. For United, there are three changes from midweek.
De Gea starts in goal.
The back four is Smalling, Ferdinand, Evans and Evra.
 In midfield Ferguson goes for Nani, Fletcher, Anderson and Young.
Up front is Rooney and Welbeck.

For City, two changes to the team that last beat Villareal, as we look forward to Mancini's 100th game in charge of City.

Hart is in net.

The back four is Richards, Kompany, Lescott and Clichy.

In midfield is Milner, Yaya Toure, Barry and Silva.

Up front, Balotelli plays behind Aguero.

On the bench for United are: Lindegaard, Jones, F Da Silva, Park Ji-sung, Valencia, Berbatov and Hernandez.

For City, their bench consists of Pantilimon, Zabaleta, Kolarov, K Toure, Nasri, De Jong and Dzeko.

That is two fairly strong benches.

Interesting from Mancini there, who has gone for Milner over Nasri, favouring the work-rate of the Yorkshire Figo over the guile of the Frenchman, and that makes sense in what could be a hectic 90 minutes. After all, you know what you'll get with Milner – with Nasri, less so.

12:45 pm. The referee today is Mark Clattenburg. He's out checking the nets and the flexibility of the corner flags. Fine head of hair on the man.

12:55 pm. In the Sky studio, there is some difference of opinion about how today will go. Gary Neville is in bullish mood – "I think the longer the game goes on, with the players they have on the bench, United won't panic."

Jamie Redknapp however fancies the visitors – "I think City will get something from the match today."

It's certainly hard to separate the sides, though City's attacking talent edges it for me.

1:05 pm. The ground is filling up, the flags are out, and the players are back in the changing rooms after some light exercises on the pitch. Not long to go now.

1:15pm. The history books will show United are the dominant force on derby day, all of which counts for precisely nothing today, as power has shifted somewhat in recent years.

1:25 pm. Out come the teams for the usual handshakes and photographs. There may even be some football shortly. The managers shake hands, though I get the impression they are not close friends – just a hunch. Perhaps Alex holds some bitterness at Mancini's ability to wear a scarf so effortlessly.

Enough of me, here we go, it's time to see who is top dog in Manchester.

KICK OFF – MANCHESTER UNITED V MANCHESTER CITY.

0:30: United kick off. Early possession for City outside United's penalty area, but the ball goes behind eventually for a goal kick off Aguero.

2:55: Young gets free down the left and wins a free kick in a dangerous position out wide as Micah Richards is adjudged to have fouled him.

3:30: The free kick hits the first defender, Silva clears but United have the ball back. The game is still settling down.

6:20: United are looking dangerous down the left with Young, and he wins a corner off Richards. The corner comes to nothing though.

7:45: Silva wriggles free and lays it square to Milner, but his long-range shot is blocked and easily collected by De Gea.

08:10: Another free kick for United down the left after a robust challenge by James Milner on Ashley Young. Milner gets a talking to by Clattenburg, though not surprisingly there was little contact on Young. Free kick from Young headed clear by Balotelli.

Ten minutes gone and United have started the game brightly with 70% possession, but there have been no chances of note.

14:00: The first bit of concerted pressure from City. A superb jinking run from Silva comes to nothing, but eventually the ball falls to Toure thirty yards out, and his shot is deflected behind for a corner. Milner over hits the resulting corner.

That was a mesmeric period of play from Silva, the ball seemingly glued to his foot as he wriggled past, around and through numerous United players in the penalty area. He could be key today.

Twenty minutes gone and the pace is frenetic, with good chances few and far between and plenty of sloppy passing from both sides. United seeing more of the ball still over all, but you feel their quick start has waned somewhat. Plenty of noise from the crowd still anyway, including just under 3000 away fans up in the corner.

21:21: GOAL! Manchester United 0 Manchester City 1. And from the game's first proper shot at goal, the visitors take the lead. David Silva plays a delightful ball down the left to Milner, who cuts the ball back past the advancing Spaniard to Mario Balotelli who scores with a sublime side foot into the far corner past De Gea's despairing dive for his 4th league goal of the season, also scoring for the 5th successive game.

22:00: Balotelli in trouble again. And a yellow card for the enigmatic Italian, who after scoring lifted up his shirt to reveal the message "Why Always Me?". Why indeed, and a rather harsh caution as he never removed his shirt. Perhaps thanking the lord will work better next time.

24:00: City's confidence is up and they are threatening more now. Aguero gets the ball wide in the penalty area but his dinked cross evades everyone. It's the away fans making all the noise, and there is plenty of frustration being showed from the home fans with each misplaced pass or loss of possession.

32:00: It's been a period without incident in the last 10 minutes. United are seeing more of the ball, but any attempts to cross are usually well-blocked by covering City players. As I type, a Young cross is deflected behind for a corner. Young takes it, Hart punches clear and Anderson shoots well from distance, but Hart collects with ease.

34:30: City have a free-kick in a dangerous position out right after Evra fouls Balotelli, but Silva's kick goes over everyone.

36:00: Rooney finds space 30 yards out, but his shot is straight at Hart.

36:30: Free kick for City after a nasty tackle on Silva by Anderson, who somehow escapes a caution. Balotelli's resultant free kick hits the wall and is cleared.

38:14: Almost a great chance for United. Welbeck feeds Rooney down the left channel, but his control lets him down which forces him wide.

39:12: Young loops a deep cross to Rooney who cuts the ball back to an unmarked Evans, but he completely miskicks and the chance is gone.

39:50: Aguero finds space in the area but his shot is blocked. That was a decent chance for City, with United's defence all at sea.

40:21: Yellow card for Vincent Kompany, who is adjudged to have hauled back Welbeck as he attempted to run onto a through ball.

40:50: Anderson fires a shot wide of the goal as the ball breaks to him just outside the area.

45:00+1: And that is half-time, and one moment of class separates the sides after a hard-fought 45 minutes low on clear-cut chances.

Half-time analysis: Naturally Manchester City will be the happiest at half-time, in a close match short on clear chances. United have had more of the ball, and probed without much success, but you get the feeling that City have a few chances in them when this game becomes stretched, and have the players to take advantage.

I'm hearing there will be no changes at half-time, so both managers happy to stick with what they have. No reason for big tactical changes at this point.

SECOND HALF: And we're off for the second half, and a fascinating 45 minutes await. How will the champions respond to going behind? City get the half underway.

46:00: **BIG, BIG MOMENT IN THE GAME.** Early second-half drama at Old Trafford and a **RED CARD for Jonny Evans**. Balotelli takes a return pass from David Silva that would have put him through on goal, but Evans drags him back and that is him off. Big advantage to City now, and all of Alex Ferguson's plans go out of the window.

47:40: It is a free kick for City too, though it was very close to being a penalty. Balotelli fires the free kick straight into the advancing wall.

50:00: Micah Richards goes charging into the penalty area and is barged off the ball by Anderson, but Mark Clattenburg is not interested. It's a close call.

53:00: Richards finds himself in the area again, but ends the move with a wild shot over the bar.

53:40: Chance for United. Fletcher squares for Young, whose appalling shot is sent straight back to him by the defending Milner, but it bounces off Young and flies wide.

56:40: Smalling shot deflected behind for a corner. United are still pushing forward with ten men.

59:30: GOAL! Manchester United 0 Manchester City 2: The same three players combine beautifully once more to double the visitors' lead. Milner finds Silva on the right of the area, he holds up the ball before setting Milner free, who squares across the goal for Balotelli to slam the ball home from close range. United have a mountain to climb.

61:00: Yellow card for Anderson for dragging Aguero back in midfield.

63:00: Silva shot deflected wide for a corner.

64:10: Almost three as Silva sends in a dangerous cross form the left, but Smalling is alert and clears the danger.

65:00: Double substitution for United as they look for a way back into the match. Anderson and Nani are replaced by Hernandez and jones.

67:00: Yellow card for Evra for a robust challenge on Gareth Barry.

68:00: GOAL! Manchester United 0 Manchester City 3 – and Sergio Aguero surely puts this game to bed for City after United are ripped apart again, and are now heading for their first home defeat in 18 months. Balotelli back-heels to Milner who sets Richards free in acres of space down the right and a simple squared ball sees the onrushing Aguero fire home under pressure from Phil Jones. City are in dreamland.

That last home defeat for United by the way was inflicted by Chelsea, and was rather costly as they went on to lose the title by a single point to the Londoners. Will this home defeat have similar ramifications at the end of the season?

69:20: Substitution for Manchester City and it is two-goal hero Mario Balotelli who makes way for Edin Dzeko.

69:50: Within seconds of coming on, Dzeko almost adds a 4th. He finds space on the left of the area and his shot is deflected off Smalling and just wide. United however get a goal kick.

70:00: And some United fans have already had enough. There's no coming back from this, and some fans have decided to leave. At least they'll beat the traffic.

A crowd of 75,487 has been announced, most of which are probably wishing they had stayed at home.

73:20: And that should have been four. Silva tries to find Dzeko, it rebounds to the Spaniard just yards out but he blazes over.

75:00: Substitution for Manchester City – that's Sergio Aguero's day over, and he is replaced by Samir Nasri.

76:50: And yet another chance for City as they once more pick off United on the counter-attack. Silva sets Dzeko free, but his shot to the far post is well saved by the feet of De Gea.

78:00: Yellow card for Smalling.

80:00: GOAL! Manchester United 1 Manchester City 3: A glimmer of hope for the home side as Fletcher curls home a beautiful shot from distance. Surely it is merely a consolation goal however.

82:00: A booking for Welbeck as United desperately look for another goal.

85:00: A booking for Richards as City look to protect what they have.

86:00: Micah Richards is named Man of the Match. There have been plenty of contenders for City to be fair.

87:32: Yaya Toure bursts into the box and curls the ball just wide.

"This city is ours!" sing the City fans, and it certainly will be tonight. They are in a blue-tinted heaven right now.

88:00: Substitution for Manchester City. Aleksander Kolarov is on for James Milner, who naturally takes his time to leave the pitch. Not much need for City to time waste though, if we're honest.

89:00: GOAL! Manchester United 1 Manchester City 4. And that is that. United give away a needless corner, Barry heads on to Lescott who cuts the ball back for Dzeko to knee it in from a couple of yards. United players claim offside, but the ball was passed backwards from Lescott. That's Dzeko's 7th league goal of the season, and his 4th goal in 5 games against United.

90:00: GOAL! Manchester United 1 Manchester City 5. And it's humiliation for United now. City break again, Dzeko feeds Silva on the right of the area and he slips the ball under De Gea to complete the rout. Amazing scenes at Old Trafford, as United head for their heaviest defeat in the Premier League.

91:40: That should have been six. Silva feeds Dzeko down the left, but he blazes over a great chance from 10 yards out.

92:50: GOAL! Manchester United 1 Manchester City 6. And that is six! One of the passes of the season as Silva volleys the ball 50 yards into the path of Edin Dzeko and he surges forward and slots home to complete the abject humiliation for United. Just when the few remaining home fans thought it couldn't get any worse, it has got worse.

FULL TIME: Manchester United 1 Manchester City 6.
Mark Clattenburg puts United fans out of their misery and blows for full time. City go five points clear of United, but that almost seems a side issue. This humiliation of United will not be forgotten for a long time, and it is clear who has the bragging rights for the foreseeable future. This was a rout, and whilst

there was a succession of late goals, it really could have been more, with Dzeko and Silva missing good chances whilst Richards had a strong penalty claim. United will have to lick their wounds and come back stronger. As for City, this is some statement of intent.

The stats: the rampant visitors had 55% possession and 19 shots, 12 of which were on target. United had 12 shots, 8 of which were on target. The early domination of the blal for United soon disappeared as City took over.

As the dust settles, it is time to reflect on an amazing day at Old Trafford, as records tumbled left, right and centre. For City, it was the first time they have scored six in a Manchester derby since 1926. It equalled their biggest margin of victory in derbies and also was their joint highest score in the Premier League. For the hosts, it was their biggest Premier League defeat, their worst home loss since 1955 and the first time they have conceded six goals at home since 1930. A truly disastrous day for Alex Ferguson and his men.

Ferguson said: "It's the worst result in my history. The impact will come from the embarrassment of the defeat. It was a bad one," said United's manager. "I can't believe it."

For the United manager, there was a clear turning point in the game.
"Jonny Evans's sending off was a killer for us. With 10 men we kept attacking - it was crazy football and ended up being an embarrassment. We should have just said: "We've had our day". I believe you shouldn't bring down a man on the edge of the box. Evans is young but he should let Balotelli go through and

see what he can do. I thought with the experience we've got - Rio Ferdinand, Patrice Evra - they would have defended more but we just kept attacking. Sometimes there has to be common sense about it. It was a bad day."

"We'll come back," he added. "We usually get the show on the road in the second half of the season and that will have to be the case. I can't believe the score-line. Even as a player I don't think I ever lost 6-1. That's a challenge for me too."

As for City, I imagine their camp is rather more bullish – especially if Micah Richards is anything to go by.

"They call us noisy neighbours," he has said. "Well, here we are!"

As for City's triumphant manager, it's not surprising to hear he is keeping things grounded.

"United are still one yard above us and we can only change this if we win the title. After that it might be different but until then United are better than us. I still have big respect for United and for their squad. There are still four or five teams who can win the title and the season is long."

Come on Roberto, call Ferguson a whinger or a bad loser. We need a tasty headline.

Ah well. Mancini had plenty to say about goal hero Mario Balotelli too.

"I hope for him, and for football in general, that the day will arrive when Mario changes his mind completely because after this he will become one of the best three players in the world like Lionel Messi and Cristiano Ronaldo. The supporters like Mario because he is crazy. I love him as a guy. I don't know what has happened [over the fireworks]. The only important thing is that Mario and his friend were OK. I think Mario played very well. If we want to talk about Mario as a football player, I think we can put him in the first five players in the world. The problem is that he is young and can make mistakes."

Mancini also explained his tactics that saw Aguero, Balotelli, Silva and Milner all start, adding: "If we had played with Nigel de Jong, we would have played with only one striker and I wanted to play with two strikers. I watched three or four games United had in the last month and they conceded a lot of chances. Also we started the season with two strikers and played very well. I am satisfied because we beat United away. I don't think there are a lot of teams that can win here. This is important for our squad and I am happy for the three points, but in the end it is three points - we don't take six points."

City keeper Joe Hart also warned his team-mates to keep their feet on the ground.

"We've got to stay level headed," he said. "We're a winning side and a team of winners but you don't get extra points by winning by that margin or by beating Manchester United. You could hear the fans today and we are delighted for them. We're a unit - the players, the staff, the fans - and that is how we roll."

That is how we roll?! Not cool Joe, not cool at all. We'll let you off after that game though, emotions can affect clarity of thought. Don't go it again though.

As for Vincent Kompany, when asked if he could believe the result, he said: "Yes, I can believe it, but it was a beautiful day. Maybe we made history today, but it's only three points, we keep looking at it that way…every single player in the team did the right thing – we defended well, we won challenges, and it made the difference, it gave us a chance to then create chances for ourselves, and we took it. I felt this game was always going to go our way as we were focussed and we were sharp."

Kompany also mentioned that the team had watched the rugby World Cup final prior to the derby and the heroic performances they witnessed seems to have spurred them on.

Just had a look quickly at the analysis in the Sky Sports studio – it's fair to say (and not entirely surprising) that Gary Neville looks like a man who has just found out he has won the lottery but used his ticket earlier to blow his nose.
Basically I'm saying he doesn't look very happy.

Time to wrap things up here after a momentous day. United fans in shock, City fans in dream land, the key fact is that City go five points clear at the top, and it is just three points at the end of the day for the title favourites, though this has been some statement of intent. And having scored 33 goals in just 9 games, they are certainly looking like future champions. For United, you just know Alex Ferguson will ensure they come back stronger, and that job begins at Goodison Park next week.
For now though, this is City's time, and there will be a few sore heads in the morning. Did we see the league's best team today? I think so, but only time will tell.

Manchester City 3 Queens Park Rangers 2
May 13ᵗʰ 2012.

"I swear you'll never see anything like this ever again, so watch it, drink it in."

1:30 pm. Welcome to the Etihad, where the sun is making the odd appearance, keen to join in the fun.
So this is it. A huge, huge day for everyone concerned with Manchester City football club, who are on the verge of their first top division title for 44 years, and thus their first in the Premier League era.

The maths is easy. City simply need to match the result of their fierce rivals and neighbours Manchester United, who are away at Sunderland, to win the title.

In their way stand Queens Park Rangers, who City cannot be expected to roll over, as they would need at least a point to avoid relegation should Bolton win at Stoke City. We shouldn't forget it is a huge day for them too.

Here's a quick reminder how it looks at both ends of the table, as we move closer to what could be a truly thrilling end to the Premier League season. For the neutral, there is always an extra thrill when there are things to play for at both ends of the table come the final day. For those involved, I would suggest thrill may be the wrong word to use.

Anyway, these are the standings at the start of play;

The top of the table:

1	Manchester City	37	27	5	5	+63	86
2	Manchester United	37	27	5	5	+55	86
3	Arsenal	37	20	7	10	+24	67

And the bottom:

15	Wigan Athletic	37	10	10	17	-21	40
16	Aston Villa	37	7	17	13	-14	38
17	Queens Park Rangers	37	10	7	20	-22	37
18	Bolton Wanderers	37	10	5	22	-31	35
19	Blackburn Rovers	37	8	7	22	-29	31
20	Wolverhampton Wanderers	37	5	10	22	-41	25

Arriving at the ground, there is a huge buzz about the place, as you would expect. Plenty of nerves too, which is shown on people's faces, but plenty of confidence and nervous excitement too. If City see this through, the fans are in for one hell of a night. And there are certainly some confident fans outside the ground. Champions scarves are selling like hotcakes. Not there yet City, not there yet, though I guess it's best to be prepared.

The stakes have never been higher than this. City will be expected to win comfortably, but the pressure will be immense.

The two Manchester sides are locked on 86 points, but City's goal difference is eight better than that of United's, so United will be relying on QPR helping them out. Still, City coped with the pressure last week at Newcastle, so will be expected to today as well.

As for the fourth team in this fascinating drama, Sunderland, they have little to play for, which is good news for United.

It's been an astonishing few weeks. United seemed to have the title wrapped up, but a 1-0 defeat at Wigan started a collapse, including that incredible 4-4 draw against Everton, that sees City enter the final day in the box seat, and has seen United squander an eight point lead. It should be a thrilling day of action. First place in the league has changed hands between City and United seven times this season. Will it change one more time?

Either way, this is the 6th time in Premier League history that the league has gone to the last day, and United have been involved every time. It is only the third time in the "noughties" though, and the previous two occasions did not have the tension of today, United and Chelsea winning comfortably to secure their respective titles. Of course City could do likewise and make this an anti-climax with a routine win, but it feels different today with United waiting in the wings and City on new ground against a team with plenty to play for. Still, QPR have lost 13 of their 18 away games, and conceded on average over two goals a game. Still, Mark Hughes hasn't lost at this ground as a visiting manager.

1:45 pm. If anyone is interested, there are two Premier League trophies for days like this, when the season goes right to the wire. The real one is close to us here at the Etihad, as City are considered the more likely league winners at the end of the action. Should United pip City to the title however there is a replica that can be wheeled out at the Stadium of Light so that United can lift aloft a trophy/drink champagne out of a cup/accidentally throw a cup under the wheels of a parade bus. As for the medals, there will be no replicas. The Premier League have ordered winners medals for both Manchester teams, though of course only one set will ever be used.

1:50 pm. If City can secure victory today then it will no doubt be painted by many as having been handed to them by United's collapse, but there must surely be credit given for the way City have remained mentally strong at the business end of the season. What's more, for Ferguson's "white flag" of a line-up at the recent derby match, his team deserve little. City themselves threw away a league lead earlier in the season, but contrary to reports it was never more than five points, so for United to have blown it this late when so far away would be the biggest "Devon Loch" moment since Newcastle's results leading to Kevin Keegan's infamous breakdown over 15 years ago.

But City are not there yet. They will need to focus one more time, be professional, and get the result. They should dominate possession today, and chances will surely follow.

2:00 pm. An hour to go, and the teams are out. For City it is an unchanged line up from Newcastle, which means a team of: Hart, Zabaleta, Kompany, Lescott, Clichy. In midfield it is Yaya Toure, Barry, Nasri and Silva, and supporting Aguero in attack is Carlos Tevez.

For QPR, three City "old boys" start.
Paddy Kenny is in net, the back four is Onuoha, Ferdinand, Hill

and Taiwo. In midfield is Mackie, Barton, Derry and Wright-Phillips. Up front are Cisse and Zamora. It's Wright-Phillip's first start in two months.

2:05pm. Will the City old boys have a say in the course of the afternoon? Nedum Onuoha was at City for eight years, famously giving up on a promising athletics career to focus on football instead. He made 95 appearances for the Citizens, was loaned to Sunderland before joining QPR in a permanent deal. He was never quite considered good enough to keep down a place for City, and he could have a busy afternoon ahead of him. Lovely man too by the way.

Joey Barton needs little introduction, and he'll be providing the bite in midfield for the visitors. For all his problems and all the controversy he has created, he should get a warm enough welcome at the Etihad today, as he never gave less than 100% for the club, and for a short while was their brightest star in darker times. The home fans have other things to worry about anyway.

Then of course there is Shaun Wright Phillips, returning to the club that made him, a club for whom he still has great affection. That £21m move to Chelsea seems a long time ago, and his skill has waned somewhat since then, but having been given a rare start today, he still has the ability to cause problems – though he may struggle to see much of the ball.

For the record, there are also three ex-United players in Sunderland's team today. They're usually quite compliant though.

2:20pm. Anyway, that's all to come. The home manager has had a few words in the tunnel as kick-off approaches.

Roberto Mancini: "I think it will be a difficult game as QPR are a good team and play for relegation. We want to have control of the game, and it is important we have the same attitude as in the last 4 or 5 games. The build-up has been the same as other games."

2:30pm. In the Sky studio, there seems little doubt how the pundits see the match going. Poor QPR hardly get a mention.

Jamie Redknapp: "Surely they can't throw it away now. I can't see anything but a Manchester City win."
Graeme Souness: "You get this far, you don't blow it."
Gary Neville: "The players completely know what they're going to do today. There's no sign of fear."

2:35 pm. You wonder what Mark Hughes is thinking right now. Naturally his primary concern is that QPR stay up, and if that is how this pans out, then that will be all that matters to him. Still, it is little secret that he rather resents the way he was forced to leave City, and in an alternative universe he could have been in the other dugout, on the cusp of his greatest managerial triumph. #SlidingDoors.

Anyway, Hughes has only had a few months to turn things around, which he has done, partly. Away form has been terrible, which doesn't bode well for today, but their home form has been the complete opposite, 5 successive wins giving them a chance of staying up today.

2:40 pm. City assistant manager David Platt carries his young son Charlie on to the field to sample the atmosphere. Carlos Tevez picks up his two daughters and does likewise. Shaun Wright-Phillips is hugging everyone he meets, clearly intent on a world record.

2:55 pm. So, here we go. Can City win that title at last, a perfect present for Yaya Toure on his 29th birthday? Or can QPR stop a run of 6 successive away defeats and beat the drop? All will be revealed in the next 90 minutes. The two teams come out the tunnel, and the atmosphere is electrifying. Even the sun is out for this.

And it's not the most important point of the day, but the confetti-strewn pitch looks in excellent nick at this late stage of the season. Well done groundsman.

3:00 pm. KICK OFF – MANCHESTER CITY V QUEENS PARK RANGERS

02:50: As you'd expect City are bossing possession, and Tevez gets his first touch in the penalty area, but his shot is blocked and goes out for a corner. The corner is cleared.

05:00: The first chance for City. Aguero manages to get the ball back near the corner flag, his pass towards the edge of the area results in an air kick from Tevez, but the ball continues to Yaya Toure who slices the ball wide.

10:00: It is all City, QPR rarely venturing into City's half, but the visitors have men behind the ball and are defending well. City have had 78% possession in the opening stages.

12:00: News from elsewhere, and it's great news for the QPR fans, as Bolton fall behind at Stoke. As it stands then, QPR are comfortably staying up. Remember, if Bolton do not win at Stoke, then QPR are safe whatever happens at the Etihad.

15:00: It's still all City and Silva wriggles free on the left of the area but his fierce shot is comfortably saved by Kenny at his near post. Kenny is showing some discomfort after that though, looks like it has stung his fingers.

18:00: With a small lull in the game, my thoughts turn back to those tiny moments that could in the end turn out to be crucial should City go on to win the title. I recall Nasri's winner against Chelsea that span straight on rather than spinning wide of the goal, Evra's missed chance against the woodwork that would have put them 5-2 up against Everton, Defoe's missed sitter just before Balotelli scored a winning penalty against Spurs back in January and how exiting the Europa League may have benefitted City in the long run. When a title race is this tight, tiny moments can be crucial. Even Kolarov's late equalizer at home to Sunderland, which at the time seemed to be of little consolation, could now make all the difference.

21:00: And this will not help the nerves of the City fans – news reaches us that over at the Stadium of Light, Manchester United have taken the lead with a Wayne Rooney header. So as it stands, United are champions, but there is of course a long way to go.

23:40: A first shot for QPR. Cissé wins a free kick outside the area after a soft foul from Barry as they contest a bouncing ball, and his low shot is comfortably saved by Hart.

25:00: Shaun Wright Phillips leaps in the air to clear the ball with his head but instead it flicks off his hand. That is millimetres outside the penalty area. Silva's resultant free kick hits the wall.

28:00: It's 80% possession for City in this match now, but no goal. It's far too early for anxiety to kick in though, with a full hour of action left. Over at the Stadium of Light, Wayne Rooney has hit the bar. The match at the Etihad is going through the same loop. City pass, pass, pass, cross, clearance, City pass, pass, pass, cross, clearance.

32:45: Nasri sets up Silva, but his shot is harmlessly wide from outside the area. He rather snatched at that.

34:00: This isn't a promising sight for City. Yaya Toure is on the deck, and seems to be clutching his hamstring. He's back up for now, but it remains to be seen if he can last the rest of the match.

37:00: And the frustration is beginning to filter down from the crowd. City are passing QPR to death, but the flicks and short passes are not working, the visitors are standing resolute.

38:30: Ignore my previous post – **GOAL! Manchester City 1 QPR 0** – Pablo Zabaleta. At last, the breakthrough for City! There's an element of luck in the goal, but the City fans couldn't care less. Silva passes to Toure on the edge of the area. He moves the ball on to the onrushing Zabaleta, whose shot is saved by Kenny, but the ball loops up, hits the post and is in. Huge relief from the crowd, and QPR may have to attack now. As it stands, City will be champions.

That is Zabaleta's 1st league goal of the season, and not a bad time to score it. However, that assist from Toure is his last contribution of the season, he cannot continue, and limps off.

40:00: Nope, scratch that, Toure miraculously jogs back into the action!

41:00: It's not been a good couple of minutes for QPR fans – over at the Britannia Stadium, Bolton are level. That's not enough to send QPR down, but one more goal for Bolton would change everything. Nervy times for everyone now.

43:21: Aguero finds a rare pocket of space just outside the area, but his shot is saved low by Kenny.

43:35: And finally Yaya Toure does succumb to injury, as he goes down again. He is off, and Nigel De Jong is his replacement.

44:30: And it is terrible news for QPR fans – Bolton have come from behind to take the lead on the stroke of half-time, and it's Kevin Davies with the strike. As it stands, QPR are down.

There will be three minutes of injury time.

Half-time – Manchester City 1 QPR 0.
A half low on chances, but enthralling nevertheless, especially with events elsewhere. City are in control, and possibly just 45 minutes away from the league title. For QPR, they are staring relegation in the face. For a short while, it felt like it was slowly going wrong for City, but they've turned things around.

So, so far so good for the potential champions, though I'm sure City fans would have liked a bigger lead, because as it stands it would only take a single moment to ruin it all. The visitors have seen so little of the ball however, you wonder how they could score, but they may have to get a result today so will have to be more adventurous in the second half – and that could play into City's hands.

3:55pm: Hearing an unconfirmed rumour that captain and key defender Kompany has pulled his calf slightly in the first half. It will be a blow if he can't finish the match, though it will take some injury to keep him off the pitch.

Here we go, 45 minutes of destiny, for quite a few teams. Is this a defining half in City's history? We're about to find out, as Mike Dean gets the action underway, eventually, ensuring the game starts at the same time as at the Stadium of Light no doubt. Neither team has made any changes during the interval, so Kompany seems to be over his little pull.

SECOND HALF – MANCHESTER CITY 1 QPR 0.

45:30: Early chance for City to wrap this up. Tevez releases Clichy down the left, his cross finds Aguero but from a tight angle, Kenny bats it behind as he tangles with the post. Nasri's corner comes to nothing, as does a free-kick from the left soon after.

47:35: GOAL – Manchester City 1 QPR 1 – I have to say, I did not see that coming, and the QPR fans are delirious. It stems from a mistake, as Joleon Lescott's back header from a looping ball heads straight towards Cissé, who runs onto the loose ball and absolutely rifles the ball into the back of the net. Suddenly everything has changed – United are champions and QPR are staying up! Lescott cannot believe what he has just done, and City must start again.

Stunned silence from the home fans, but there is plenty of time to fix this. Not surprisingly, the away fans are in good spirits.

49:30: Tevez squeezes a shot away from a tight angle, but it's easy for Kenny.

51:00: A strange chance is missed by Aguero. De Jong and Barry both go for a corner, the ball breaks 30 yards out for Zabaleta, whose stinging shot is heading wide before it reached Aguero just three yards out, and his instinctive flick sees the ball loop just past the far post.

54:00: Oh my word, it is all happening now, and the end result is a **RED CARD** for **Joey Barton**! Astonishing scenes here as Barton tries to fight half the City team. It all started as Barton and Tevez tangled on the edge of the QPR area. Tevez went down clutching his face. Barton protests his innocence as City players surround him, but the linesman on the far side wants to speak to Mike Dean and Barton is off for an elbow! The reply shows he has little to complain about, though Tevez does kick out just prior to that, which is probably what prompted his outburst. Astonishingly though Barton seems intent in taking City players with him. As he walks past Aguero he kicks out at him, sending him to the ground, and City players do well not to react. Micah Richards is on the pitch to lead him off safely, but Mario Balotelli senses blood and riles Barton further. Chaos here at the Etihad, but considering his team is fighting relegation, this is absolute madness from QPR's captain, and the visitors have got a long 40 minutes ahead of them.

For good measure, replays show an attempted Barton head-butt on Kompany. Keep it classy Joey.

57:30: The end result is a free kick for City in a dangerous position. Tevez's shot is into the wall, but it falls for Nasri whose snap-shot is well saved by Kenny.

Substitution for QPR: Mark Hughes looks to tighten things up as City throw everything at the visitors, and Traore is on for Cissé.

59:20: A Tevez cross is blocked but the ball falls back to him and his stinging shot draws another excellent save from Kenny. Better is to come though, with Aguero somehow missing the easiest of chances. As the ball rebounds out, Barry heads forward, the ball appears to hit a QPR hand, Tevez prods it sideways to Aguero three yards out but his shot is straight at Kenny, who parries it and scoops the ball off the line. So, so close for City, but it remains all square.

City are throwing everything at QPR now, but cannot find the vital breakthrough. And they need to, as United remain a goal ahead at Sunderland.

Replays show a clear batting away of the ball in that earlier move by Nedum Onuoha. Lucky, lucky boy. It was unintentional by Onuoha, but his arm was well away from his body.

65:00: Astonishing! Absolutely astonishing! **GOAL! Manchester City 1 QPR 2**. Manchester City look set to throw away the title as only they can, and QPR fans are in heaven! Another City attack breaks down, and Kenny finds Traore on the left who surges down the wing and crosses perfectly onto the six yard line, and in steams Mackie to slam a diving header into the turf and past the despairing dive of Joe Hart and a back-peddling Lescott into the back of the net. City players are stunned, QPR fans are delirious.

Well that wasn't in the script. City came out for the second half with a lead and having had all of the ball in the first half. QPR have managed to pick up a red card since then and yet somehow City have managed to throw it all away. For City fans the clock will suddenly speed up now.

What can City do now? Their worst nightmares are coming true, and they have 25 minutes to turn this around. They need two goals to clinch the title, unless Sunderland do them a favour, and to be honest there's more chance of Kylie Minogue popping round my place tonight for a hug and some heavy petting.

67:00: City are beginning to look desperate now, and Silva shoots well over from distance. Roberto Mancini appears to be shouting random obscenities at his players – he is stunned as the rest of us, and there is not a lot he can do apart from hope the skill of his expensive side can make the difference at some point. QPR though have everyone behind the ball, at all times.

68:30: City need a Plan B, and Mancini thus makes a change. Edin Dzeko is on for Gareth Barry.

70:00: Another cross, another headed clearance. The clock is ticking down.

71:20: Another corner finds the head of Tevez, but Kenny tips the ball over easily enough.

71:40: Another corner is punched half-clear but falls for Zabaleta 15 yards out, centrally. His shot though is superbly blocked – it's another corner.

73:00: Tevez slaloms into the area, but slices his shot horribly wide. That sums up his day. Twenty one attempts for City, but just the solitary goal.

It's the last-chance saloon for City and Roberto Mancini, and Mario Balotelli is about to come on. It is wave after wave of City attacks now, with the ball permanently in the QPR half, but the visitors are defending for their lives.

75:00: And here he comes. That's the end of the action for Tevez, and with a last throw of the dice, on comes Mario Balotelli. Tevez hasn't had a great day to be honest, though he did manage to provoke Joey Barton into a red card, so it's not all bad.

And a **substitution for QPR** also, with Jay Bothroyd coming on for Bobby Zamora.

76:00: Huge cheers emanate from the away end, which can only mean one thing – Stoke have equalized at the Britannia Stadium against Bolton, and QPR are looking safer than ever.

77:20: So close for City, Aguero scoops the ball in and Dzeko shoots at the near post, but somehow Kenny keeps it out as he dives in the opposite direction. Another corner is City's only reward.

78:40: Balotelli shoots from wide, and Kenny parries it clear.

82:40: Dzeko finds space on the left of the area, but his shot is so bad it goes out for a throw-in. It is looking truly desperate for City now.

84:00: Dzeko gets on the end of a cross, but it's a simple save for Kenny. City need a miracle here now, or at Sunderland, or both.

86:40: Yet another corner, but Silva's ball goes over everyone, and that is surely that. United are still one up at Sunderland.

87:30: And just what City didn't need. The QPR players have just realised the pitch has two halves, and have a short spell of possession in attacking areas. This winds down the clock further.

I tried to avoid looking, but there are some truly miserable faces in the home crowd.

90:00: Possibly one final act of defiance from Paddy Kenny kills City's hopes. Another corner, Balotelli gets his head on it, but somehow Kenny keeps it out. And of course it's another corner, the save rebounding off a QPR player and going behind.

There will be five minutes of injury time. The smallest chink of light for City.

91:14: Oh hello! GOAL – Manchester City 2 QPR 2. Well well well. Surely too little too late, but there is some gossamer-slim hope for the blue half of Manchester, as Dzeko gets on the end of another Silva corner and this time heads home for the equalizer. Mixed applause from the crowd (and a few pumped fists too) as the players rush back to their own half. City have just under four minutes to complete the greatest escape act in living memory.

Astonishing scenes here as City pour forward again. It's quite simple now – one goal wins the title.

93:00: It is over at Sunderland – United have won, so City simply HAVE to score.

93:20: GOAL! MANCHESTER CITY 3 QPR 2!!!!!!!!!!!!

GGHDSFDSFDSFDSFDSFDSDSXXCDSS!!!!!!

OH.MY.GOD. UTTERLY ASTONISHING. In the dying moments of the game, up pops Sergio Aguero to give City their first title in 44 years after an unbelievable two minutes. The ball was played forward to Baloteli by Aguero on the edge of the area after Nigel de Jong had advanced up the pitch, and Balotelli laid it back to Aguero as he turned and fell, Aguero skipped past one prone defender before slamming the ball home past Kenny. And off he goes to celebrate the greatest moment in this club's history, as City dig themselves out of the world's greatest hole. The place is rocking, I have never seen anything like this. What an escape, what a turnaround.

Shirt off for Aguero, twirled around his head, and a huge scrum of City players pile on him on the far side of the pitch.

Football! Bloody football!

And it's important to relay the news that **QPR ARE SAFE**. Bolton could not get the three points they needed, so both sets of fans will be celebrating tonight!!

And I think the QPR team knew they were safe by the time Aguero scored, due to signals from the away bench and the noise from their own fans.

Just seen a replay of Joe Hart's reaction to that goal. Needless to say he was quite happy with what happened and with no one to hug he ran around aimlessly, his face so joyful I was worried it might explode.
And Mancini too, whose jigs of joy on the pitch will be replayed for many a year. Less so Kolo Toure, who seemed rather unimpressed with the greatest moment in Premier League history.

Let's not forget, this game is not over. QPR to kick off, but they have nothing to play for. I doubt they'd want to urinate on City's parade.

Yellow card for Aguero for that goal celebration by the way. I'm saying nothing.

95:10: And indeed, QPR chip the ball out from the kick off. Joe Hart has it now, he has no intention of doing anything with this ball, and the QPR players have no intention of challenging him. Surely two very happy sets of fans are seconds away from beginning the celebrations in earnest.

95:35: FULL TIME – Manchester City 3 QPR 2: AND THAT IS THAT! MANCHESTER CITY ARE THE PREMIER LEAGUE CHAMPIONS!

QPR STAY UP.

Absolute euphoria on the pitch from the City players, and the QPR team aren't too downbeat either. Pure adrenalin on the faces of the home players as they embrace anyone they can find. Plenty of home fans getting in on the celebrating too with the inevitable pitch invasion. You can barely see any green now as thousands of home fans revel in an astonishing day.

And the man who almost ruined it all, Djibril Cissé, seems pretty happy and keen to join in with the home team's celebrations! He's good friends with Samir Nasri, amongst others.

The teams go off, but they will be back.

Manchester City had 44 shots to QPR's three. 81% possession to 19%. 19 corners to 0. Three goals to two, though, is the only stat that matters.

"Staggering, just staggering! He's won the league with 90 seconds of stoppage time to play. It's just the most extraordinary scenario you could have dreamt up. Where does football go from here?" Premier League TV commentator Peter Drury sums up a rather remarkable few moments in Premier League history.

Wow. Struggling to take all that in. I've aged 40 years in 93 minutes. You'd have to go back to 1989 I reckon to see a league finale quite this thrilling and dramatic. City have only dropped two points at home all season, but they were determined to make life as difficult as possible for themselves.

So what a journey for City this season, from the moment it all began on a Monday night as Sergio Aguero announced himself with two fantastic goals, Swansea were swept aside, many more were too thereafter, but a mid-season and a last-day wobble almost ruined it all, but they got there in the end – just.

The heart's still pounding, I think I need a stiff drink*. There will be some celebrations going on in the dressing room right now, involving copious amounts of a certain French fizzy drink, but they will no doubt be back out on the pitch soon for some more formal celebrations and a few fireworks.

(*please drink responsibly)

Though probably not any time soon. There are still fans on the pitch getting all emotional and kissing the turf, and the tannoy announcer is sounding increasingly desperate in his pleas for the pitch to be cleared. He has now threatened the cancellation of the trophy presentation if people don't return to their seats. I'd say that's rather unlikely, there'd be riots in the streets, and rightly so, though I do not condone violence or destruction of property.

Slowly but surely, the pitch is clearing. No rush, but I was supposed to have clocked off twenty minutes ago.

Just watching that final goal again on a loop – I don't think I will ever get bored of watching it, though Manchester United fans might disagree. Interesting to note that Aguero could easily have gone down when the challenge came in and got a penalty, which would have led to heart-stopping levels of stress for the home fans but credit to him, as he had only one thing in mind – hitting the back of the net. Which he did.

Balotelli would probably have been the man to take that penalty. Good lord.

Roberto Mancini has just been interviewed in the tunnel whilst wrapped in the Italian flag. He looks remarkably calm and unflustered considering what has just happened. I was secretly hoping he would pop out for a chat in just his underpants, drenched in champagne with a tie round his forehead. Ah well, here's what he had to say:

"We have beaten United two times, we have scored more than them and conceded less so we deserve it. I never gave up. It was a crazy finish to the game and the season but the best team won the title."
"When I said the title was over a few weeks ago it was because I wanted to take the pressure off," Mancini explained. "I was sure we would have another chance. We now need to improve and I am very happy because for an Italian to win the title here in England is fantastic for all Italian people."

And a bit more. "This is an incredible moment. We wanted this title and we deserve to win this title. This is for all our supporters, the club, the chairman and the owner. This is the perfect finale for a crazy season."

Legend status for Roberto Mancini is assured amongst the City fans, but as David Platt has just explained to a gaggle of journalists, he will have forgotten about this tomorrow and will go again. Can the Italian make City the country's best team over the coming years? He stands a good chance, but you know United (and others) will come back strongly next season.

5.20pm: Back in the tunnel, Mancini is greeted with a kiss by his father Aldo. Mancini Snr has made the journey from Italy despite health problems and inevitably there are tears from both men.

Almost time to wrap things up here, as the players are back out, with families in tow. A stage has been hastily erected, and as confetti is blasted into the air, Vincent Kompany lifts the Premier League trophy, and the players and staff enjoy the title win. Now the celebrations can REALLY begin. I hope you enjoyed the day half as much as we did.

MANCHESTER CITY - PREMIER LEAGUE CHAMPIONS 2011/12

About The Authors

Simon Curtis

The irony of having Manchester City attract your attention in 1974, just after the end of the club's greatest trophy run in history, did not become fully apparent to Simon Curtis until some 35 years later, when he realised he had followed his club through a lifetime of joyless lack of achievement. The last five years may have made up for that somewhat, but – to paraphrase slightly the infamous banner at City matches– he's seen things others will never see. He now pens his thoughts on City in a thrice weekly ESPN column and other musings across a range of websites, magazines and blogs, including Down The Kippax Steps.

Howard Hockin

Howard Hockin has been writing about Manchester City since he had brown hair, which is a long time ago. A City supporter since approximately 1982, he has been musing on his club's ups and downs for over a decade, starting with contributions for City's only remaining fanzine, King of the Kippax. Since then he has written for a wide range of websites and fanzines, and has released four season review books, a charity City book and is most proud of once sneaking on the reserve City trophy parade bus. You can find his ramblings at standingalone.co.uk and on twitter (@howiehok34).

12946578R00100

Printed in Poland
by Amazon Fulfillment
Poland Sp. z o.o., Wrocław